Decades before cornbread, shrimp and grits, and peach cobbler were mainstays on menus everywhere, Edna Lewis—"the first lady of Southern cooking" (NPR)—was pioneering the celebration of seasonal food as a distinctly American cuisine.

In this timeless cookbook, Miss Lewis (as she was almost universally known) shares the recipes of her childhood, spent in a Virginia farming community founded by her grandfather and his friends after Emancipation, as well as those that made her one of the most revered American chefs of all time. Interspersed throughout are personal anecdotes, cooking insights, notes on important Southern ingredients, and personally developed techniques for maximizing flavor.

In Pursuit of Flavor is a modern classic—and a definitive compendium of Southern cooking at its very best.

ALSO BY EDNA LEWIS

The Taste of Country Cooking

The Edna Lewis Cookbook

The Gift of Southern Cooking (with Scott Peacock)

IN PURSUIT
of
FLAVOR

IN PURSUIT

of

FLAVOR

Edna Lewis

✦

WITH MARY GOODBODY
FOREWORD BY MASHAMA BAILEY
ILLUSTRATED BY LOUISA JONES WALLER

✦

ALFRED A. KNOPF   NEW YORK   2019

THIS IS A BORZOI BOOK PUBLISHED BY ALFRED A. KNOPF

www.aaknopf.com

Knopf, Borzoi Books, and the colophon are registered trademarks of
Penguin Random House LLC

Library of Congress Cataloging-in-Publication Data
Names: Lewis, Edna, author. | Goodbody, Mary, author. | Waller, Louisa Jones,
illustrator.
Title: In pursuit of flavor / Edna Lewis with Mary Goodbody ; foreword by
Mashama Bailey ; illustrated by Louisa Jones Waller.
Description: Updated edition. | New York : Alfred A. Knopf, 2019. |
Includes index.
Identifiers: LCCN 2018035278 | ISBN 9780525665510 (hardcover : alk. paper)
Subjects: LCSH: Cooking—Virginia. | Cooking, American—Southern style. |
LCGFT: Cookbooks.
Classification: LCC TX714.L66835 2019 | DDC 641.59755—dc23 LC record
available at https://lccn.loc.gov/2018035278

Case photograph by John T. Hall
Case design by Carol Devine Carson

Manufactured in the United States of America
Published October 6, 1988
Updated Edition, March 28, 2019

CONTENTS

FOREWORD

MY FATHER IS FROM New York City, but my mother was born in Waynesboro, Georgia. I am the oldest of their three children, and at an early age, I was given the responsibility of taking care of my siblings while my parents worked nights and continued their education. We were reared as New York City kids who played in our father's mother's backyard, or on concrete, or in subway cars. But there were times when we would go home, to where my mother was born.

Waynesboro is a small town with pretty much just one of everything. My grandmother's house was yellow with a big front porch. Geneva and Wille C. West, my mother's parents, would often sit outside and wave at the neighbors passing by. East 9th street, where they lived, was a busy place; there was a flower shop across the street next to the funeral home; a candy store close enough to the house for us children to walk there alone; and a gas station where we would buy pints of ice cream to survive the summer heat. Farmers pulled up in their pickup trucks to sell the day's bounty. Fishing poles hung from the porch ceiling of my grandmother's house and out back, for my grandfather to use every weekend. Even as a young child, the excitement of evenings filled with fresh trout dinners and laughter with my cousins gave me a sense of peace. I was often jealous of their quieter lifestyles when we went home to the city. I so badly wanted a deep Southern accent when I returned to school in the fall . . . but then I'd become immersed in city life once more, until we returned again to our family in the South.

Growing up, I never had dreams of becoming a chef. I thought I would be a doctor, a poet, or a physical therapist. As I became older and learned about good food through my parents, I began to enjoy cooking. Being in the kitchen made me happy. I even loved grocery shopping, as did my my paternal grandmother, Margie Bailey, and so we used it as a way to bond. Margie was a

great cook who entertained often and had every casserole dish to show for it. Still, I never had professional culinary ambitions—I only wanted to learn to cook well enough to keep my family and friends coming back for more, and to stay connected to my roots.

It wasn't until after college, and after a few false starts, that I ended up in culinary school. That's where I first heard of Miss Edna Lewis. During the first few weeks of class, my chef instructor gave us a writing assignment: "Find a chef that you admire."

I was stumped. I wasn't familiar with popular chefs at the time. Even though I was in culinary school, I never had lofty goals of owning a fancy restaurant with fancy food. But I did some research, and what I learned became one of the most important professional questions I have answered.

Finding your culinary mentor is not an easy thing to do. Some people search for decades to connect with someone who shares a basic level of understanding and background. Miss Lewis was that person for me. It took me years to realize that a cookbook would help me find my north star. The more I learned about Miss Lewis, the more I understood that food in a restaurant doesn't need to be fancy, just good and wholesome, like the food my grandparents cooked in Waynesboro. Having a real connection to our food, something more than a supermarket flier or a frozen bag of peas, was a missed fortune.

With *In Pursuit of Flavor,* Miss Lewis showcases her expertise and techniques by taking us on a journey through her childhood. She brings to life the entire farmland as it was seen by someone who lived off the land. She picks fruits and vegetables and shows us how to prepare them for the cupboard.

She shows us how to preserve the bounty of the season for later. She takes us to the river and creeks to teach us about the local catches.

My restaurant, The Grey, in Savannah, is only a hundred miles from where my mother grew up. *In Pursuit of Flavor* helped me to put my own menu into perspective. We use Miss Lewis's distinctions of country living—along with my own childhood memories of the South—to seek out the freshest ingredients, and her book helps us understand how to process and present these ingredients to our guests in a truly southern way.

I never had the opportunity to meet Miss Lewis, but through her food, I like to think that I've come to know her very well. From her, I've learned about my own likes and cravings. I've learned what people once had to do in the country to survive. There has been a reemergence of traditional ways and cooking good old-fashioned food in this country, and it started with Miss Lewis many years ago. She was at the forefront then and three decades later, her voice continues to lead the way for chefs young and old in their pursuit of flavor.

Mashama Bailey

INTRODUCTION

I LEARNED ABOUT COOKING and flavor as a child, watching my mother prepare food in our kitchen in Virginia. She took great care with the food she
fed her large family and our assorted guests and I suppose I just naturally
followed her example. In those days, we lived by the seasons, and I quickly
discovered that food tastes best when it is naturally ripe and ready to eat.

I grew up in Freetown, a small farming community in Orange County,
Virginia, which was founded by my grandfather and his friends shortly after
his emancipation from slavery. Living in a rural area gave my mother the
chance to cook food soon after it was picked. We also canned and preserved
the fruits and vegetables from the gardens and fields. The pickles, relishes,
chutneys, jams, and jellies added colorful balance to nearly every meal, their
tart or sweet flavors offsetting milder ones.

I feel fortunate to have been raised at a time when the vegetables from
the garden, the fruit from the orchard, and the meat from the smokehouse
were all good and pure, unadulterated by chemicals and long-life packaging.
As a result, I believe I know how food should taste. So now, whether I am
experimenting with a new dish or trying to recapture the taste of a simple,
old-fashioned one, I have that memory of good flavor to go by.

There are so many ways to get the best out of vegetables; for instance, com-
bining tomatoes (ripened at home if they are off season) with cymling squash,
pumpkin with onion and bacon, cooking sweet potatoes with lemon, and
boiling corn in its husk. I always keep a bit of country ham around, the way
my mother did, or streak-of-lean, to perk up greens or to use as a complement
to any number of dishes. The way you use herbs is important, I've found;
some are better dried than fresh. How you cut them and when you add them
to the pot make a difference. Cooking fish fillets or chicken breasts in parchment is a wonderful way to seal in delicate aromas; braising in a clay pot

keeps meat moist. I've worked out a method for making an intense-flavored stock by searing chopped-up bones and flesh together, then cooking them quickly. Bones always give flavor, and I often bake sweet-smelling fish with the bones in, as well as roasting fowl whole, or rabbit, or a suckling pig on occasion, each with its own dressing that sets off the taste of the particular meat. And when it comes to baking there are so many tricks I've discovered, such as using the right flours, making your own baking powder (to avoid that chemical taste), learning to *listen* for signs of when a cake is done, using bits of frozen butter for one kind of pie crust, pure leaf lard for another. These are just some of the techniques I have developed to get the best flavor from the foods we find today.

In recent years I have been heartened by the growth of farmers' markets all across the country, where farmers can sell their products to city people, who more and more are looking for fresh, organically grown vegetables, fruit, meat, and poultry. I have also witnessed promising changes in the ways supermarkets display and sell food. While I continue to believe that we refrigerate too many things and rely too much on the freezer, knowing when to use modern appliances to your advantage is important to a good cook. Every summer, for instance, I pick or buy as many ripe berries as I can find, certainly more than I can eat. It's no bother to freeze them and very easy to preserve them, which means I have the taste of summer far into the winter—a gooseberry sauce for some roast fowl or currants for a pie.

I have noticed that as people get older, they're apt to complain that food simply does not taste as good as it used to. I don't believe this has to be true, and that is why I have tried, in working out these recipes, to give you all kinds of suggestions to make food taste the way you remember it. For those who are too young to remember, I hope the recipes will be a welcome introduction to good food simply and lovingly prepared. One of the greatest pleasures of my life has been that I have never stopped learning about good cooking and good food. Some of the recipes here are old friends, others are new discoveries. All represent a lifetime spent in the pursuit of good flavor.

IN PURSUIT
of
FLAVOR

One

FROM
THE GARDENS
AND
ORCHARDS

Sweet Green Peas and Explorer Potatoes in Cream Sauce

Fresh Green Peas with Vidalia Onions

Sweet Green Pea Soup

Creamed Scallions

Morels in Oil

　Olive Oil

Wild Watercress Cooked in Pork Stock

Watercress Soup

Cooked Greens

Sautéed Spinach

Long-Cooked Green Beans

Canned Green Beans in Pork Stock

Cold Tomato Soup with Basil

Tomato and Onion

Tomato and Cymling

Wilted Lettuce Salad

　Tossed Green Salad

Dressing for Tossed Green Salad

Salad of Whole Tomatoes Garnished with Green Beans
and Scallions

　Basil

Mayonnaise

Summer Hot Vegetable Dish of Green Beans, Carrots, Leeks,
Tomatoes, and Sautéed Mushrooms

　Fresh Boiled Corn on the Cob

Eggplant Stew

Eggplant

White Eggplant Slices with Tomato and Onion Sauce

Grilled Eggplant

Grilled Eggplant with Marinated Tomatoes and Artichokes

Whipped Cornmeal with Okra

Grits

Potatoes Baked with Virginia Ham

Fried Potato Cakes

Leek and Potato Soup

Steamed Leaves of Leek

Sautéed Wild Mushrooms

Pumpkin with Sautéed Onions and Herbs

Baked Sweet Potatoes with Lemon Flavoring

Beef Barley Stew

Beef Soup with Wild Mushrooms

Black-eyed Peas and Other Dried Beans

Black-eyed Peas in Tomato and Onion Sauce

Thirteen-Bean Soup

White Beans and Lentils in Tomato Sauce

Cabbage and Sauerkraut

Stewed Sauerkraut

Red Rice

Coconut Rice

Sautéed Bananas

Braised Chestnuts for Stuffing or Serving with Vegetables

Purée of Chestnuts

WHEN I WAS GROWING UP, we ate only what was ripe and fresh at the moment, which, as the spring and summer passed, changed from week to week. This meant that if you were not quick, you could miss a favorite summer treat and would have to wait all year before you could enjoy that good taste again. Beginning with the first spring thaw, we foraged for wild greens and a little later in the year hunted berries and nuts. We planted the garden carefully so that it produced a steady supply of vegetables during the warm months, and picked fruit from the orchards only when it was ripe and sweet.

In this chapter, I have tried to follow the seasons, beginning in the spring with a recipe for tender green peas and Vidalia onions. You will not find many recipes for fruits and berries here—they appear later in the book when I discuss jams, jellies, preserves, and desserts. What you will find are vegetables with good flavor that I think have stood the test of time or can be cooked so that their true flavor comes through. The recipes bring out these natural flavors, showing off each vegetable to its best advantage: sweet peas, eggplant, tomatoes, green beans, leeks, and other vegetables found in many gardens. None of the recipes calls for underripe (the "baby" vegetables so popular nowadays) or undercooked vegetables. I don't think you get the true flavor of a vegetable if it is partially cooked. If a vegetable is meant to be eaten raw, then it should be raw, but if not, it should be honestly cooked.

I have tried to use vegetables in combination with others that are naturally ripe at the same time. If you eat a vegetable when it has been grown under all the right conditions, including reaching maturity at the right time of year, it tastes as good as can be. I think it is important to keep this in mind—which is why I am delighted that so many cities have established farmers' markets where local farmers can sell their produce. At the farmers' markets, not only can city dwellers buy farm-fresh fruit and vegetables—and often meat and fish, too—but also the small farmers have outlets for the crops they so lovingly grow and tend.

In New York, where I have lived most of the time, I go to the Union Square Greenmarket two or three times a week. I have gotten to know a number of the farmers and often strike up conversations with them about various fruits and vegetables. I recall talking to a young man who had bought land with damson plum trees on it. He was not sure what to do with the plums and so he asked me. As I was explaining all the wonderful things you can do with the old-fashioned fruit, a lady standing nearby decided she would try some damsons, too. I know another farmer who grows twenty-five different varieties of lettuce and almost every week in the spring and fall, he brings a new kind to try. These lettuces are just delicious and have nearly always been picked the day before, or early that morning, before dawn, by the light of the tractor. He also grows old-time root vegetables such as salsify.

I have found all different types of potatoes at the Greenmarket. To me, nothing tastes better than a freshly dug potato from a summer garden. When it comes to autumn's sweet potatoes, I prefer the light yellow ones to the orange-fleshed ones called yams. The lighter ones are drier, not as sweet, and really taste good, although they disappear quickly in the fall, since not too many farmers grow them.

There is so much variety at farmers' markets you never tire of strolling among the stalls and trying different fruits and vegetables, comparing the flavor of one with that of another sold by a different farmer. Regardless of claims to the contrary, the produce is far superior to that sold at supermarkets—even supermarkets where the vegetables are displayed loose and pretty—because supermarket buyers are constrained to buy from large commercial growers through big distributors. I have never felt that a vegetable grown in an open field tastes as good as one grown in a small garden. Our garden, when I was a child, was a pampered piece of soil outside the kitchen window, nurtured with compost, ashes from the wood stove, and manure from the barnyard. A garden gets better every year—the weeds and plants are chopped up and turned back into the earth, compost is added, and sometimes natural lime, too, is mixed with the soil to sweeten it. The soil, so well cared for, naturally becomes deeper and richer every year.

Some herbs grown in a garden or a pot on the windowsill are much better than dried packaged ones, but there are a few I prefer dried—thyme, rosemary, and oregano, for instance. When I buy dried herbs, I always date the jar or box and store it in the refrigerator tightly closed. They get stale after a couple of months and ought to be replaced. I rely on a small group of herbs to bring out the good flavor of foods, herbs such as fresh parsley, chervil, basil, and tarragon. I always chop these herbs fine when cooking with them as the chopping releases their oil and juices and brings out their intense flavor. When I am garnishing with herbs, I just snip them with scissors over the dish or pot. This does not release their juices and so they never overwhelm.

I also use garlic a lot to enhance the taste of food. I do not believe that yesterday's crushed garlic is any good—always start with fresh garlic. How it is handled alters its flavor. For instance, if you are adding garlic to a marinade, I suggest laying a peeled clove on a plate and scraping the flesh so that it turns into soft mush. For some reason, this tastes stronger and sweeter than chopped garlic. When you are cooking chopped garlic, add it to the pan after the onions are partly cooked and never let it burn. Its flavor will be ruined.

Beyond the garden is the orchard. When I was a child, nearly everyone had at least a few fruit trees, all bearing different fruit, ready to be plucked at their peak of ripeness for pies, preserves, or simply to eat on the walk back to the house. Small orchards are disappearing. They were planted by another generation for us to enjoy, and if you have the space, think about planting some fruit trees for the next generation.

And beyond the orchard are the fields and woods, where wild things grow—watercress, mushrooms, strawberries, blackberries, grapes, and nuts. Perhaps it is because of the natural, undisturbed compost that nurtures them year after year, or perhaps it is because they grow only where the soil, light, and humidity are right for them, but wild things never fail us. They always taste good, which is why if you see only a handful of wild nuts or a cupful of berries, you should pick them. They have a flavor nothing else has. If you transplant a wild plant to the garden it will never taste the same.

Sweet Green Peas and Explorer Potatoes in Cream Sauce

Explorer potatoes are tiny, elongated potatoes with brown skins. They are so small they do not have to be peeled or even cut, and their texture is a little better than that of other small potatoes. Unless you grow them yourself they are difficult to find, but they are in some specialty stores in June, July, and August—which is when a lot of people like to eat potatoes anyway because they are so fresh.

I add chervil to this recipe because I love its flavor and never cook peas without it. Fresh chervil has the aroma of freshly mowed grass and a sweetness that improves the flavor of peas. I remember peas being much sweeter and tenderer when I was young, and even when I grow them myself nowadays they are not as good as they were. Frozen petits pois peas are as reliable as any for this recipe and many others.

SERVES 4

3 cups shelled peas (about 3 pounds peas in pods)	1 tablespoon sugar
	1 bunch chervil with leaves and stems
1 cup tiny explorer potatoes	1 cup heavy cream
½ teaspoon salt	1 tablespoon butter

Rinse and drain the peas. With a knife scrape the potatoes clean and cook them in a saucepan of boiling salted water to cover. Remove them after 15 minutes, when they are not quite done. Plunge the peas into another pan of boiling water seasoned with the sugar. Add the chervil and do not cover. Boil rapidly until the peas are done and the hulls are tender. Drain, return them to the pan, and add the potatoes. Pour in the heavy cream and cook gently without boiling for 15 to 20 minutes, until the potatoes are tender and the rest of the meal is being finished. Add the tablespoon of butter. Stir and serve hot, garnished with leaves of finely cut chervil.

Fresh Green Peas with Vidalia Onions

I have only known about these sweet onions for ten years or so, but ever since I first tasted them I have loved them. While Vidalia onions are available until November, they are most plentiful in May and June. The onions grow in the region of Vidalia, Georgia, where the soil is just right to produce a sweet-tasting onion; if the same seed is planted elsewhere, the onions are sharp. I think the flavors of sweet spring peas and sweet onions go together perfectly and this combination has become one of my favorite dishes—as nearly anyone who I have cooked for in the last few years knows quite well. The best time to cut the center from the steamed onions is after they have cooled. The onion may fall apart if you try to cut the center from it while it is hot.

SERVES 4 TO 6

4 to 6 medium Vidalia onions
1 pound fresh peas, shelled
1 tablespoon sugar
7 or 8 stalks chervil, with leaves
1 good tablespoon butter
⅔ cup heavy cream
Salt

Put about 3 inches of water in a 2-quart steamer. Peel the skin off the onions and score the bottom with an X, then place in the steamer. Cover tightly and steam over medium-high heat for about 20 minutes, until the onions are tender. Take them from the pan and let them cool on a plate before cutting out the centers with a sharp knife to make a cup for the peas.

Pour ¾ cup of water into the saucepan and bring to a rapid boil. Add the peas, sugar, and chervil. Cook, uncovered, until the peas are tender. Drain, remove the chervil, then add the butter and shake the pan to coat the peas evenly with butter. Stir in the cream and season to taste with salt. Place an onion cup on each plate and spoon a generous amount of peas into the center of each. Spoon a little more around the outside of the onions. Reheat before serving.

SWEET GREEN PEA SOUP

Soup made with tender garden peas tastes quite different from pea soup made with dried peas. It is not as thick and the blending of peas and chervil gives it a crisp, fresh flavor that holds up whether the soup is served hot or cold. I like to garnish the light-tasting soup with small dabs of unsweetened whipped cream.

SERVES 4

1½ pounds sugar snap peas in the pods
5 cups water
½ cup packed sprigs chervil
1 teaspoon sugar
½ teaspoon freshly ground black
   pepper

Salt
1 cup julienned romaine lettuce
½ cup unsweetened whipped cream
   (optional)

Rinse the peas, drain, and shell them. Heat the water to boiling in a large saucepan, and add the peas and shells. Stir in the chervil, sugar, and pepper, and cook briskly, uncovered, for 15 minutes, until the peas are tender. Cool the soup and pour it into a blender. Blend until liquefied, then push the soup through a sieve to hold back any undesirable pieces from the peas and the pods. Add 1 teaspoon of salt and taste for seasoning. Stir in the romaine lettuce and heat the soup, if you plan to serve it hot. If you plan to serve it cold, chill it until ready to serve. Spoon a little whipped cream in each soup bowl just before serving, if you like.

CREAMED SCALLIONS

Growing up, we would sow onion seed in the garden and then thin a lot of them out before their bulbs got too big. We chopped them up, sautéed them in bacon fat, poured in heavy cream, and ate them for breakfast. This recipe is not quite as rich as that, but uses scallions in a way that tastes just delicious. In my opinion, they are an underused vegetable and taste almost as good today as they did years ago. I buy scallions that are about the size of a pencil but if they are a little thicker they still taste good.

SERVES 5

About 30 medium scallions
3 tablespoons cold water
⅔ cup heavy cream

¼ teaspoon chopped garlic
1 tablespoon finely cut parsley, for
    garnish

Clean the scallions by removing the roots and a bit of the tops. Put the water in a heavy pan with a cover along with the scallions. Cook, covered, until the scallions become tender but remain green, about 5 minutes. While the scallions are cooking, put the heavy cream in a shallow 8-inch skillet along with the chopped garlic. Boil the cream hard enough to reduce it to 5 tablespoons of sauce. Remove the scallions to a warm, flat dish, spoon the reduced cream over them, and sprinkle with the parsley. Serve hot.

MORELS IN OIL

I think this is my favorite way to serve wild mushrooms. The flavor is heightened by the garlic and oil. I cook only morels this way because I do not think the texture of other mushrooms would hold up in the oil. They are a wonderful garnish with cold chicken, game, or veal, or a Bibb or romaine lettuce salad.

SERVES 4

   1½ cups cold water
   ½ teaspoon salt
   6 large blond or gray morels
   1 clove garlic, finely chopped
   Olive oil

In a 1-quart saucepan, bring the water to a boil, and add the salt. Add in the morels and cook briskly, covered, until tender, 10 to 12 minutes. Remove from the burner. (Save the liquid for a sauce or stew.) Place the morels in a deep dish. Add in the garlic and enough olive oil to cover. Cover, and refrigerate until ready to serve. It is best to let marinate for a few days.

Olive Oil

Overall, I think olive oil is pretty good these days. For cooking, I do not use extra-virgin olive oil, the kind that looks green, which I use for salad dressings. For most cooking purposes, I find that mild-flavored olive oils, such as the moderately priced brands sold in supermarkets, are just fine. I sometimes put olive oil in mayonnaise but just as often use vegetable oil because it tastes lighter. When I am at home, I juggle different oils around—I will try walnut or hazelnut oil in salad dressing, for example—but I always come back to olive oil, which is my favorite.

WILD WATERCRESS COOKED IN PORK STOCK

The flavor of wild watercress is very different from the flavor of the watercress you buy from greengrocers. It tastes really peppery, so peppery that a little in salad is all most people want. When you cook it, though, it takes on a different, milder flavor—but it is still peppery. Unless you pick it yourself, wild watercress is hard to find, although every now and then you will see it sold in farmers' markets and small greengroceries. It isn't hard to recognize in the fields. Wild watercress grows in small bunches, flat out like a plate, in lowlands and near streams. You find it when the weather is still very cold but after the snow has melted. As soon as it gets warmer out, the watercress goes to seed. You may use other watercress in the recipe—I sometimes do—but the flavor will be less intense.

SERVES 4

3 pounds wild watercress (or 10 to 12 bunches cultivated watercress)

2 quarts pork stock (see page 20)

Salt and freshly ground black pepper (optional)

Prepare the watercress by cutting the leaves away from the root stem. Plunge into a large pan of water to get rid of the sand and soil that usually adheres to the cress. Rinse until there is no sand in the bottom of the pan.

Heat the pork stock to boiling and add the watercress. Cook, simmering, for 1 hour, or until the desired tenderness is reached. Drain and serve as you would other greens. Season with salt and pepper if needed.

WATERCRESS SOUP

This pretty green soup makes a very good first course, although you rarely see it. It has an almost "new" taste and the addition of unsweetened whipped cream adds to the texture and goodness of the soup and enhances the subtle flavor of the watercress.

SERVES 4 OR 5

3 bunches watercress
6 cups chicken stock
½ cup finely chopped onion
Salt and freshly ground black pepper

1½ cups heavy cream (not ultra-
    pasteurized)
Unsweetened whipped cream

Open the watercress bunches and wash with lots of water. Drain well and set aside 2 cups of the leaves. Chop the whole watercress coarsely, then chop the leaves. Put the chicken stock in a 4-quart pot and heat. Add the chopped whole cress and onion, and simmer for about 15 minutes. Strain the soup and discard the watercress and onion. Season to taste with salt and pepper, and add the heavy cream and the reserved chopped leaves. Mix well and set aside until ready to serve. When ready to serve, reheat without boiling. Garnish each bowl with a teaspoon of unsweetened whipped cream and serve.

COOKED GREENS

Greens are a dish that most Southerners would walk a mile for. They were part of the daily meals and believed to be very good for you. If a neighbor fell ill during the winter, friends would search the countryside to uncover some wild cress growing in the lowlands along streams. After it was found, the cress was quickly washed and cooked and taken to the sick for nourishment. Both wild and cultivated greens are prepared the same way, except for spinach and kale, which usually are not cooked with pork. Wild greens include lamb's quarters or pigweed, poke salad, dandelion, purslane, wild mustard, and watercress. These were found from early spring until late in the fall, with cress, which was sometimes uncovered beneath the winter snow, being the exception. The garden yielded kale, mustard greens, turnip and beet tops, rape, and collards.

It is popular to cook a mixture of greens together. Some are quite bitter and benefit from being plunged in boiling water for a minute or two to temper their flavor. This is rarely necessary with freshly picked greens, but those sold in greengroceries and supermarkets might be a little old and need this treatment. Remove large, sinewy stems and ribs and tear oversize leaves into big pieces.

The best meat for the stock is smoked shoulder, but bacon and streak-of-lean (see page 124) are acceptable. It is the flavor of the smoked meat, not the fat, that makes the greens taste so good. When I was growing up in Virginia, every house had a round tray on the table holding bottles and jars of oil, vinegar, mustard, salt, pepper, and sugar so that everyone could season their own greens.

SERVES 4

1 pound cured smoked pork shoulder, bacon, or streak-of-lean	3 pounds greens, such as mustard, rape, or collards
3 quarts water	Salt and freshly ground black pepper to taste

Cook the pork and water in a 5-quart pot for 1½ hours or more, until the meat is very tender. Remove the meat from the stock and discard. Add the greens. You will have to pack them in but they cook down quickly. Cook

(recipe continues)

over medium-high heat for about 25 to 30 minutes. Do not cover the pot or the greens may turn dark. Be careful not to undercook the greens, which is as bad for them as overcooking. I always test them for doneness after 15 minutes although they sometimes need 20 minutes of cooking. During cooking, season them with salt and black pepper. Lift them from the pot, shake off excess liquid, and serve hot.

SAUTÉED SPINACH

Sautéed spinach is a delicious vegetable dish, and if you have not tried it, you really should. The spinach should be very fresh and clean and completely dry. I suggest washing it well after discarding the thick stems and then drying it in a salad spinner. Spin dry only a handful at a time and then leave the leaves out to finish drying in the air.

SERVES 4

2½ pounds fresh spinach	½ cup (1 stick) butter

Trim the stems from the spinach. Soak it in lots of cool water to wash away the sand. Shake the water from the spinach leaves and dry them completely. They must be totally dry when they are cooked.

Melt the butter in a wide, heavy frying pan. Add the spinach all at once and stir continuously for about 3 minutes, until the spinach is limp and shiny. Take the frying pan from the heat, drain off any liquid in the pan, and serve the spinach hot from the stove.

LONG-COOKED GREEN BEANS

Nowadays people laugh at the idea of cooking beans for an hour or more, but in the old days, before all the chemical fertilizers, beans were slower growing and tougher skinned and needed to be simmered on the back of the stove for a long time. Everybody cooked them this way and I still do when I find the right kind of string bean. What is more, I have never really liked undercooked vegetables. If you want to try cooking beans this way, or if you grow your own beans, look for Kentucky Wonder beans, which are a little longer and have thicker skin than other string beans.

SERVES 8

1½ pounds dry-cured country pork
shoulder, ham, or bacon
2 quarts cold water
3 pounds Kentucky Wonder whole
green beans, ends trimmed and
strings removed

Salt, if needed, and freshly ground
black pepper
Finely chopped parsley, for garnish

Wash off the pork well and put it in the water. Bring to a boil, and simmer gently for at least 1 hour, until the flavor has been extracted from the meat. Remove the cooked pork and add the beans. Bring to a boil, then turn the heat down, and simmer gently for at least 1½ hours, until the flavor of the pork has been imparted to the beans. Season to taste with salt (if needed) and pepper. When the beans are done, remove them from the heat and set aside until ready to serve. Reheat and serve hot, garnished with finely chopped parsley.

Canned Green Beans in Pork Stock

A lot of people can the green beans they grow in their gardens, but these beans are apt to taste rather bland. So here is a way of making canned green beans—whether your own or store-bought—taste really good and not just like canned beans. The recipe is similar to long-cooked green beans, but these only have to cook for 30 minutes or so, while the long-cooked beans cook for more than an hour. I always can green beans because I feel that good, fresh food that has been preserved tastes far better than vegetables grown in the off-season or sold by commercial packers. When I can beans, I follow the instructions that come with the Ball jars.

SERVES 4

½ pound cured smoked pork shoulder   1 quart canned green beans
     or bacon   Salt and pepper to taste
1 quart cold water

First make the pork stock. Wash the pork, removing any residue. Make a number of slices in the meat without separating it into pieces. Put the pork into a 2-quart saucepan with the cold water. Set this on a burner and cook slowly for 1 hour, until tender. Remove the meat from the boiling stock. Open and drain the quart of canned beans, then add them to the stock. Simmer the beans in the stock for 30 minutes or more. Season to taste and set aside until ready for use. Reheat and serve hot. These beans are more flavorful when cooked and reheated before dinner.

Cold Tomato Soup with Basil

This soup can be made any time of year, providing you have ripened the tomatoes. I use tomatoes nearly every day and so, except in the summertime, I suggest buying them about two weeks before cooking and leaving them alone to ripen. Put them on the windowsill or on the kitchen shelf—not in the refrigerator. When you buy the tomatoes, they are usually pink or red, which does not mean they are ripe. After about two weeks they become deep, deep red—the color completely changes. They still feel firm (but not rock hard) and their flavor is good, although never as good as in the summer.

This really is my favorite tomato soup, and I serve it hot with cheese straws when the weather turns cool. I never seem to have a problem finding fresh basil, and as for the oregano, I like it dried better than I do fresh anyway. Somehow oregano and a few other herbs seem weaker when they are fresh. If you do not add baking soda to the milk, it will curdle.

SERVES 4 OR 5

4 pounds tomatoes, peeled, seeded, and cut into pieces	Salt
1 cup water	2 tablespoons sugar
1 teaspoon dried oregano leaves	2 cups milk
Freshly ground black pepper	2 cups heavy cream
2 sprigs basil, each with 4 or 5 leaves	1 cup basil leaves, torn into small pieces
½ onion, chopped	1 pound tomatoes, peeled, seeded, and cut into strips
1 teaspoon baking soda	½ cup unsweetened whipped cream

Put the 4 pounds tomatoes, water, oregano, ½ teaspoon of pepper, basil sprigs, and onion in a 4-quart enamel or stainless steel pot, and place over medium heat to cook. Watch carefully from the beginning to see that the mixture does not burn. Stir often and cook for about 25 minutes, then add the baking soda and mix well. Remove from the heat. Remove the basil sprigs and press the soup through a sieve into a bowl, or blend to liquid in a blender then pour into a bowl. Mix thoroughly and cool. When cold, stir in 2 teaspoons of salt, sugar, more pepper if needed, milk, heavy cream, and the torn-up basil leaves. Fold in the strips of tomato, correct the seasoning, and serve chilled. Garnish each serving with a teaspoon of the unsweetened whipped cream.

TOMATO AND ONION

I cook this combination of vegetables in a heavy frying pan for a long time so that it simmers down to a thick consistency. The red tomatoes sprinkled with the green parsley really add color to a plate holding chicken, lamb, or beef. I use this as a garnish on lots of different dishes and just love the way it tastes with meat. While it is cooking I sort of shake the pan every now and then, and when it is done, I drain off the excess olive oil. But you have to use the full measure of olive oil, since this is what gives the dish such good flavor. Sometimes I use the drained-off olive oil in something else because it tastes so much of onions.

SERVES 4

½ cup olive oil

2 medium onions, peeled, quartered, and sliced medium thick

2 pounds tomatoes, peeled, seeded, and cut into strips

1 teaspoon salt

½ teaspoon freshly ground black pepper

Finely cut parsley

Heat a large, heavy skillet until hot. First put the olive oil in the skillet and then the onions, and cook, stirring, for 4 or 5 minutes, until the onions are softened. Add the tomatoes and salt and pepper and mix well. Turn down the heat and let the mixture simmer for about 1 hour, or until the moisture has evaporated from the sauce in the pan. Drain off the excess olive oil. Check for seasoning, spoon the mixture into a serving dish, and sprinkle generously with finely cut parsley.

TOMATO AND CYMLING

Cymling, which is also called patty pan squash, was the only squash I knew about when I was young. Sometimes we would steam it but mostly we would dip it in flour and fry it just like chicken. We would even have it fried for breakfast. In this recipe, the tomatoes and basil give it good flavor and the squash adds its own texture.

SERVES 4

⅔ cup olive oil

3 pounds tomatoes, peeled, seeded, and cut in pieces

6 or 7 fresh basil leaves

5 small cymling (patty pan) squash, cut into 1-inch-thick wedges

Salt and freshly ground black pepper

Heat a heavy skillet until hot and then put in the olive oil, tomatoes, and basil leaves. Add the cymling and mix well. Cook until the cymling are tender but not overdone, about 10 minutes. Season with salt and freshly ground black pepper and remove the basil leaves. Serve hot.

WILTED LETTUCE SALAD

In early spring, lettuce was the first vegetable in the garden, and it was always a delight to prepare a quick, simple wilted lettuce salad using crisp greens picked early in the morning while the dew was still on the leaves. The sharp, strong dressing of vinegar and bacon fat mingled deliciously with other vegetables served at the meal, too.

SERVES 4

1 cup cider vinegar
Scant ¼ cup sugar
1 teaspoon salt
1 teaspoon freshly ground black pepper
6 slices bacon
Crisp greens, such as romaine, cress, arugula, purslane, Bibb, or any

other, washed and completely dried
½ cup small basil leaves, or 4 or 5 big leaves
2 tablespoons chopped fresh parsley

Mix the vinegar, sugar, salt, and pepper in a small bowl. Cook the bacon in a stainless steel or enamel frying pan, until crisp. Lift the bacon from the pan and drain on paper towels. Discard all but 3 tablespoons of bacon fat, which should be left in the pan.

Break up enough greens for 4 servings and put the leaves in a bowl along with the basil. Set the bowl near the stove. Crumble the bacon and have it ready. Raise the heat to high under the pan with the bacon fat and add the vinegar mixture. Stir and heat to boiling. Immediately pour the hot dressing over the greens and toss. Sprinkle the crumbled bacon and chopped parsley over the salad and serve it at once.

Tossed Green Salad

I think the best time to serve a tossed salad is after the main course and before dessert. I like to put a good goat cheese and bread on the table, too, and perhaps open another bottle of wine when I serve salad. I find this point in the meal is a relaxed and friendly time. I like to combine different greens in the salad, some bitter, some sweet. I particularly like arugula, Bibb and Boston lettuce, early romaine, black-seeded Simpson, purslane, and cress. Since there are so many greens available today at the farmers' markets and greengrocers, you should experiment with them yourself and come up with a mixture you like. For all this, the dressing is most important. When I mix a dressing and get the good flavor I am after, I immediately draw a line on the jar indicating the depth of the vinegar and of the oil. I then use this as my guide the next time. Be careful when measuring the salt; an oversalted dressing is awful but an undersalted one can taste flat. I make fresh dressing every day rather than making a lot at once and storing it in the refrigerator.

DRESSING FOR TOSSED GREEN SALAD

I suggest making this in a jar or glass cruet. For a variation on the dressing, omit the onion, garlic, and sugar, and replace them with a tablespoon of grated raw potato. I like to scrape the onion because cutting an onion in half and scraping it with a spoon releases the liquid and the full essence of the onion's flavor.

½ cup cider vinegar

1½ teaspoons salt

½ teaspoon freshly ground black pepper

Scant ½ teaspoon sugar (optional)

½ teaspoon dry mustard

1 teaspoon scraped onion

1 clove garlic, peeled and cut in half

⅔ cup olive oil

Put the vinegar, salt, pepper, optional sugar, mustard, onion, garlic, and olive oil in a pint jar with a lid, and shake until the salt is dissolved. Remove the garlic. Shake again just before dressing the salad.

Salad of Whole Tomatoes Garnished with Green Beans and Scallions

This salad is better in the summer when the tomatoes are at their best, but is good all year long if you find some good greenhouse tomatoes and let them ripen on the kitchen shelf for a few days or longer. In the summer, vine-ripened tomatoes (such as Jersey tomatoes if you happen to live in the area) are not as expensive as hydroponic or imported tomatoes and this gives some people the impression they are not as good! Or shoppers shy away from buying sun-ripened tomatoes because they may look yellow near the stem end, which is only natural. During the summer there is no reason *at all* to buy tomatoes that are wrapped in plastic or grown in a greenhouse. Buy the tomatoes that have been grown in a garden or field near where they are sold.

When I make the salad, I dip the whole, peeled tomato in the dressing and leave it for 15 minutes or so. I also marinate the green beans and scallions in the dressing. This way, when I am ready to assemble and serve the salad, I simply lay the vegetables on the lettuce and do not have to add any more dressing. The vinaigrette I use here is a little sweeter than the salad dressing on page 26 and has no garlic or onion.

SERVES 5

2 teaspoons salt

½ pound whole green beans

VINAIGRETTE DRESSING

⅔ cup olive oil
⅓ cup apple cider vinegar
1 teaspoon salt
1 teaspoon sugar

½ teaspoon freshly ground black pepper
2 teaspoons finely chopped parsley

10 to 12 scallions, trimmed, some green top left on
5 whole tomatoes, peeled and cored
5 leaves Boston or romaine lettuce

About ½ cup Herb Mayonnaise flavored with basil (see page 29)
1 tablespoon finely torn basil

(recipe continues)

Have ready a large saucepan of boiling water. Add the salt and the beans. Cook rapidly, uncovered, for 10 minutes, or until the beans are tender and no raw taste remains.

Meanwhile, make the vinaigrette. Put all the ingredients in a screw-top jar and shake well.

Drain the beans, put them in a dish, and pour ⅓ cup of vinaigrette over them.

Put the scallions in just enough boiling water to keep them from scorching—about ½ cup. Cook briskly for 4 minutes, shaking the pan to ensure that all the scallions are scalded and remain glossy green. Drain them, put in a deep dish, and spoon 4 tablespoons of vinaigrette over them.

Put the tomatoes in a deep bowl and pour the rest of the vinaigrette over them. Marinate for 15 minutes, stirring around occasionally to make sure they are well coated with dressing.

To assemble, place a lettuce leaf on each plate. Drain the tomatoes and set them on the lettuce. Garnish around the tomatoes with green beans and scallions. Then fill the cavity of each tomato with mayonnaise. Sprinkle finely torn basil over.

BASIL

Basil is easy to grow and tastes very good on fresh vegetables and in soups and sauces. I prefer the plants with the tiny leaves, which you can grow in a pot or in the garden. The small leaves can be pinched from the plant and used without being cut—cutting sometimes darkens basil leaves. If you use large leaves, try to tear them whenever possible. In Virginia, purple basil seems to grow everywhere, and I like it just as much as green basil. It looks pretty, too.

MAYONNAISE

After you make mayonnaise, you can add any herb or combination of fresh herbs to a cup of mayonnaise and mix them together in the blender to make a smooth, well-flavored sauce to serve with chicken, fish, or cold vegetable dishes such as tomato aspic. I suggest about 3 tablespoons of herbs for 1 cup of mayonnaise, but you can adjust this amount to a desired strength. For another flavor, substitute parsley for the basil in this recipe.

MAKES ABOUT 2 CUPS

2 egg yolks
1 teaspoon dry mustard
1 teaspoon salt
1½ cups mild olive oil or corn oil

1 tablespoon freshly squeezed lemon juice
1 tablespoon white wine vinegar

Put the egg yolks, mustard, and salt in a 2-quart bowl. Beat well with a wire whisk for 2 minutes. Add a drop of oil and continue to stir. Keep adding the oil, drop by drop, until the mayonnaise begins to thicken. Combine the lemon juice and vinegar. Alternately add the oil and the vinegar and lemon juice, whisking continuously, until the mayonnaise is thick and smooth and all the oil is incorporated. The mayonnaise will keep for a few days, covered, in the refrigerator.

HERB MAYONNAISE

Measure 1 cup of mayonnaise from the bowl and put it in a blender. Add 1 tablespoon each of torn basil leaves, chopped chervil, and chopped tarragon, and blend just for a minute to chop the basil further. Try to use the herb mayonnaise right away.

Summer Hot Vegetable Dish of Green Beans, Carrots, Leeks, Tomatoes, and Sautéed Mushrooms

Over the years, I have developed the habit of making big vegetable dishes in the summer, as I often have no time to cook a big meal with meat. When you sauté the mushrooms, let them brown a little—the browned taste is delicious against the steamed or boiled vegetables. This dish is especially pretty if you select vegetables of equal length. You may serve it as a side dish, but with the garlic cream sauce it makes a substantial main course. This sauce is very simple. It is delicately flavored with garlic and just delicious spooned over most vegetables. You have to boil the cream so that it will thicken to the right consistency, but boiling it does not change its flavor, as it does the flavor of milk.

SERVES 4

1 bunch carrots, trimmed and scraped
6 leeks, trimmed and washed
1 pound green beans, trimmed and washed
7 tablespoons butter
½ pound mushrooms, cleaned and thickly
    sliced
½ teaspoon finely chopped garlic
½ lemon
Freshly ground black pepper

GARLIC CREAM SAUCE

1½ cups heavy cream
¼ teaspoon scraped garlic

Salt and freshly ground black pepper
    to taste

½ teaspoon salt, or more to taste
2 or 3 ripe tomatoes, peeled, seeded,
    and cut into julienne pieces

1 tablespoon finely chopped parsley or
    basil

Cook the carrots and leeks in separate pots, covered, in boiling salted water for 15 minutes. Cook the beans, uncovered, in boiling salted water for 7 minutes. Drain all the vegetables and keep warm until needed.

While the vegetables are cooking, heat 6 tablespoons of the butter in a large pan until sizzling hot and then add the mushrooms and garlic. Cook the mushrooms fast so that they do not develop any juice, about 5 to 6 minutes, or until brown. Squeeze a little lemon juice over the mushrooms and add some freshly ground pepper.

Meanwhile, make the sauce. Put the cream and garlic in a wide skillet set over a medium burner, and bring to a boil. Boil rapidly until reduced to ⅔ cup—about 3 to 5 minutes. Season to taste.

Heat another large skillet until hot and add the remaining 1 tablespoon of butter. Sear the drained carrots, leeks, and beans to take away the boiled taste, adding about ½ teaspoon of salt. Take a flat round or oblong dish and heap the seared vegetables in the center. Scatter the mushrooms on top and garnish the sides of the dish with the tomatoes. Sprinkle the whole dish with finely chopped parsley or basil. Serve with Garlic Cream Sauce.

FRESH BOILED CORN ON THE COB

Summertime is just nothing without boiled corn on the cob. When I was younger, we would have corn and tomatoes for lunch, nothing else. And for dinner, corn would be a separate course, which we would eat after the main part of the meal when the dishes were cleared away. After all, you really can't eat anything else if you are concentrating on corn.

If the corn is real sweet, I can eat it without butter, but usually I like lots of butter and salt and pepper, too. My favorite kind of corn is white corn and the two best, I think, are Country Gentleman and Silver Queen, although Silver Queen sometimes is a little off flavor. For yellow corn, I like Golden Bantam, which you do not see much anymore, Golden Midget, Truckers Favorite, Kandy Corn, and just plain Golden. Still, it was not until I was a teenager that I even ate sweet corn. Before then all I had eaten was field corn, which has a flavor all its own that is just delicious. The kernels are meatier than sweet corn kernels. Sometimes we would bake field corn in the oven, first removing the outer leaves of the husk and leaving only the inside leaves. The corn would be a little bit crispy and very flavorful since no water ever hit it.

It is best to cook sweet (or field) corn the same day it is picked, and the sooner the better. Sometimes this is not possible, since the corn field may be far away from the kitchen. If I cannot cook corn the same day, I set the whole ear in a pan of water to keep it from drying out. I like to boil corn in the husk because I think it adds flavor and holds in moisture. To do so, pull back the husk to the bottom of the cob but do not detach it. Take off the silk and then pull the husk up over the ear of corn again. Tie it closed and drop the corn in boiling water. Simmer the corn for 10 minutes and turn off the heat. Let the corn rest in the pot for 15 to 20 minutes until you are ready to eat it. Lift the corn from the pot, peel off the leaves, and wrap the corn ears in a tea towel to keep them warm at the table.

EGGPLANT STEW

This recipe was mailed to me about forty years ago by a French engineer who had dined at the Café Nicholson. Since I first tried it, it has been one of my favorites. Surprisingly, after three hours' cooking the vegetables still hold their shape because you don't stir them. The stew is soft and delicious—a nice dish to make when you are home all afternoon. Make it with white, purple, or any other color eggplant.

SERVES 4

½ cup olive oil
2½ onions, chopped
5 tomatoes, peeled, seeded, and
    chopped
2 small zucchini, thinly sliced

1 medium to large eggplant, peeled,
    quartered, and coarsely chopped
½ teaspoon salt
½ teaspoon freshly ground black
    pepper
Chopped parsley

Heat the olive oil in a heavy-bottomed saucepan. Sauté the onions until they are translucent, but not browned. Add the tomatoes, and cook over low heat for 15 minutes. Add the zucchini and eggplant, and season with salt and pepper. Cover, and simmer on the lowest heat for 3 hours. You should check the stew to make sure it isn't sticking; if it seems to be, put the pot over a flame-tamer. I prefer cooking this dish on the stove, but it can also be baked in a 300°F oven for about 2 hours. When done, spoon off any excess oil. Sprinkle the chopped parsley on top and serve hot or cold.

EGGPLANT

I prefer white eggplant simply because it rarely tastes bitter, as purple eggplant sometimes does. I discovered white eggplant at the Greenmarket. I later found out from my Ghanaian friends that it is called "garden egg" in Ghana, which made sense to me—its shape and color make it resemble a large white egg. When I cook with white eggplant, I never salt it because it never tastes bitter. White eggplant is a little rounder than the purple and is glistening white with a bright green stem. It tastes real sweet, does not have much seed, and has a finer, less spongy texture than purple. Today the markets are stocked with eggplants in all different colors: light green, pink, purple, and white. All taste good but it is a sensible idea to salt all eggplant except white to avoid bitterness. Any kind of eggplant can be cooked in different ways as an appetizer, side dish, or main course.

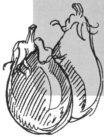

White Eggplant Slices with Tomato and Onion Sauce

The flavor of white eggplant is cool and delightful and I often sauté it quickly in oil or bacon fat, but this method of baking it in the oven is just delicious and makes a good appetizer or side dish, hot or cold.

SERVES 4

½ cup olive oil
1 large onion, sliced and cut up
1 clove garlic, scraped
4 good-size tomatoes, peeled and
chopped
1 teaspoon salt

½ teaspoon freshly ground black
pepper
½ teaspoon dried thyme leaves
1 large white eggplant, cut into ½-inch
slices

Heat the olive oil in a large frying pan over medium heat. Add the onion and garlic, and sauté for 5 minutes, stirring to keep them from browning. Add the chopped tomatoes and simmer, uncovered, until the mixture has cooked enough so that the liquid is evaporated, about 1 hour. Take from the heat and season with salt, pepper, and thyme. It should be highly seasoned.

Preheat the oven to 350°F.

Oil a large roasting pan or cookie sheet and arrange the eggplant slices on it. Using a slotted spoon, spoon the tomato sauce over each slice of eggplant and bake for 25 to 30 minutes, until the eggplant is tender. Serve hot or cold.

GRILLED EGGPLANT

This is such an easy and delicious way to serve eggplant, especially good in the summer when the eggplant is fresh and tomatoes are at their best. I like it served cold with wedges of seasoned tomatoes, steamed Vidalia onion vinaigrette, a dry goat cheese, and crusty yeast bread.

SERVES 4

1 or more large white eggplants
½ teaspoon salt
½ teaspoon freshly ground black
    pepper

1 clove garlic, crushed
1 cup mild olive oil

Remove the stem, rinse the eggplants, and cut in half. Cut the halves lengthwise into halves again and slice into 1½-inch-thick pieces. Add the salt, pepper, and garlic to the olive oil. (Make sure the garlic is well crushed.) Mix well and then coat the eggplant pieces with the oil and let them rest for a minute.

Lay the eggplant pieces on a preheated grill and cook for 3 to 4 minutes on each side. You can serve the grilled eggplant warm or cold.

GRILLED EGGPLANT WITH MARINATED TOMATOES AND ARTICHOKES

I developed this recipe specifically for purple eggplant because it is so plentiful in the markets and often is the only kind available. I chose a young vegetable with very firm skin that had been picked the day before, and because it was so fresh I did not salt it. It did not taste the least bit bitter, and although I do not know for certain if its freshness had anything to do with this, perhaps it did. Summer is the best time for this appetizer, when the vegetables are so delicious and the grill is going with meats and fish.

Four ½-inch slices firm goat cheese, cut from a log

3 or 4 sprigs fresh rosemary

Olive oil

1 teaspoon salt

½ teaspoon freshly ground black pepper

1 clove garlic

Twelve ½-inch wedges peeled ripe tomato

Twelve ½-inch wedges purple or white eggplant

1 pint Jerusalem artichokes, peeled and julienned (about 2 cups)

3 tablespoons Vinaigrette Dressing (see page 27)

4 slices white bread, toasted and cut into rounds

4 sprigs fresh basil

Put the goat cheese and rosemary sprigs in a small glass or ceramic bowl and pour enough olive oil over to cover. Let the goat cheese marinate for 4 to 5 hours or overnight at room temperature.

Mix 1½ cups of olive oil, salt, and pepper in a large bowl. Peel the garlic clove and scrape it with a sharp knife into pulp. Add the garlic pulp to the bowl and stir until the salt disappears. Spoon some seasoned oil over the tomato wedges and set them aside.

Spear each eggplant wedge with a fork or skewer and dip each piece into the olive oil. Lay them on a platter to marinate while the grill is getting hot. When the grill is nice and hot, grill the eggplant for about 10 minutes, turning often to cook on all sides. Remove the eggplant from the grill, and take the wedges from the skewers. Set aside on the platter and sprinkle with just enough of the seasoned olive oil to keep the eggplant from drying out. Let the eggplant wedges cool to room temperature before serving.

Toss the artichokes with the vinaigrette and marinate for a few minutes.

Preheat the oven to 250°F.

Lay the toast rounds on a cookie sheet and top each one with a slice of goat cheese. Heat them in the oven for about 10 minutes, until the cheese is warmed through but not cooked. Put one toast round on each serving plate and spoon the marinated artichokes and tomato wedges around or over them, however you desire. Arrange the grilled eggplant on each plate and garnish with a sprig of basil.

WHIPPED CORNMEAL WITH OKRA

I first was served this dish by a friend from the Caribbean, and it quickly became one of my favorite ways to eat cornmeal. The okra dissolves in the hot cornmeal so all you have is its flavor—not its slippery texture.

SERVES 4

2 cups water
6 pods fresh, tender okra
1 cup white cornmeal
½ teaspoon salt
½ cup (1 stick) butter, cut into pieces

Bring the water to a gentle boil in a 3-quart saucepan and cook the okra for about 10 minutes. Lift the okra from the water with a slotted spoon and set them aside. Raise the heat so that the water is boiling briskly. Add the corn-meal in a thin, steady stream, stirring all the while to prevent lumping. Never let the water stop boiling. Add the salt and the okra, still stirring, and cook for 10 to 12 minutes. Remove from the heat and add the butter a piece at a time, stirring after each addition until all the butter is incorporated. Keep stirring until the okra has practically disappeared and the cornmeal is light and fluffy. Taste for seasoning and serve the cornmeal hot.

GRITS

Grits, which are dried ground corn, are famous as being Southern. They usually are eaten with ham, poached eggs, sausages, fried chicken, or fish. Although butter is often the only flavoring added to grits, I like to eat them with shrimp paste. To cook them, pour boiling water over the dried grits and then set them over simmering water in a double boiler for an hour to give them time to come to the proper consistency. Stir them every now and then as you go about making the rest of the meal.

SERVES 4

¾ cup grits   ½ teaspoon salt
4 cups water

Heat the water to boiling in the top of a double boiler and add the grits. Set the top of the double boiler over simmering water. Cover, and cook for 1 hour, stirring occasionally. Mix well and serve the grits hot.

POTATOES BAKED WITH VIRGINIA HAM

Potatoes are one of the few vegetables that are good in all seasons—although in the summer when they are freshly dug from the garden, they taste especially delicious. Besides the familiar varieties such as Idaho, russet, and cobbler, there are new kinds of potatoes in the markets. Most have similar flavor and some, such as small explorer potatoes, can be added whole and unpeeled to soups and stews. Recently I found a yellow potato at New York's Greenmarket that had a slightly different texture and a heartier flavor than most white potatoes. I have also tried blue-skinned potatoes, which look pretty and taste just about the same as any other potato. Use any white potato for this recipe, which makes a good supper dish.

SERVES 4

½ clove garlic	2 tablespoons finely chopped
2 tablespoons melted butter	parsley
5 medium potatoes, peeled and sliced	2 cups julienned Virginia ham
Salt	2 cups heavy cream
Freshly ground black pepper	½ cup bread crumbs

Preheat the oven to 350°F.

Crush the garlic and stir it with 1 tablespoon of the melted butter. Rub an 8-inch square pan, 2 inches deep, with the butter. Layer the potatoes in the pan and season them lightly with salt, pepper, and some chopped parsley. Next, sprinkle a handful of ham over the potatoes. Repeat the layering until the pan is full and the top layer is potatoes. Add the cream, which should be nearly level with the top layer of potatoes.

Cover and bake for 45 minutes. Toss the bread crumbs with the other tablespoon of melted butter. Take the pan from the oven and distribute the bread crumbs evenly over the potatoes. Continue baking, uncovered, for 5 to 10 minutes, until the bread crumbs are browned.

FRIED POTATO CAKES

I usually make potato cakes from leftover whipped potatoes, but in case you do not have leftovers, I have included instructions for whipping about 4 cups of potatoes. The cakes are fried in butter until the exteriors are nice and crispy and the insides still soft. I prefer Idaho potatoes for whipping—they have a dry texture that whips up light.

SERVES 4

3 medium potatoes, peeled and
   quartered
Salt
½ cup milk or half-and-half
7 tablespoons butter

½ teaspoon freshly ground black
   pepper
1 cup flour seasoned with salt and
   pepper

To whip the potatoes: Put the potatoes in a 2-quart saucepan and cover with cold water. Bring to a boil and add 1 teaspoon of salt. Cook briskly for 25 to 30 minutes, until done. Drain and set aside to dry.

Heat the milk in a small saucepan but do not let it boil. Remove from the heat and add 4 tablespoons of butter. Mash the dry potatoes in a bowl, and when the butter is completely melted, add to the potatoes and beat with a stout spoon. Stir in the pepper and taste for seasoning. Whip the potatoes until light and smooth and then spoon them into a shallow baking dish. Let cool and refrigerate until ready to make the cakes.

Take the potatoes from the refrigerator and let them warm up a bit at room temperature. Pinch off a piece of the firm mashed potato and shape it into a round about ½ to ¾ inch thick and 2 inches in diameter. Spoon the flour into a shallow bowl and dip the potato cake in the flour to coat both sides and the edges. Lay the cake on a sheet of wax paper while you form 8 or 9 cakes in all.

Heat 3 tablespoons of butter in a heavy skillet until it foams. Just as the butter begins to brown, add the potato cakes. Fry the cakes over medium-high heat until golden brown. Turn the cakes over and fry until crisp on both sides. Serve immediately or keep warm until ready to eat.

Leek and Potato Soup

The best thing about making this soup is the wonderful aroma that fills the kitchen. Cooking the leeks and potatoes without water produces the delicious smell and also gives the soup its true flavor. Because leeks are so sandy, you must wash them well. I usually cut the green leaves off about ½ inch from the white part, then I make a cross about an inch deep into that green end and turn them upside down in water. They open up—and the sand floats out.

SERVES 6

5 tablespoons butter
2 large leeks without green part, chopped into small pieces
2 large potatoes, peeled and sliced
6 cups chicken stock (see page 74)
Salt and freshly ground black pepper to taste
2 cups hot milk
2 cups hot heavy cream
⅓ cup snipped chives

Put the butter in a 4-quart heavy-bottomed pot and heat until the butter melts and begins to reach the foaming stage. Add the leeks and potatoes and mix well. Cover loosely. Do not add any water or liquid yet. Heat on a medium burner just high enough to keep the leeks and potatoes from burning or sticking. When hot, cover tightly and cook until a steam develops that sends out a great aroma. After about 15 minutes, add the chicken stock. Cover, and simmer for about 1 hour.

Remove from the burner, cool, then put into the blender with the salt and pepper, and purée. Add the hot milk and cream, correct the seasoning, and serve hot; garnish each bowl with a teaspoon of cut-up chives. The soup is delicious cold, and when it is served cold, you do not have to heat the milk and cream. Wait until the soup is chilled, then stir in the milk and cream.

STEAMED LEAVES OF LEEK

I really do not know why more people haven't thought of cooking the green tops of leeks. I decided to try one day when I was making leek soup and could not bear to throw away the healthy-looking greens. When I steamed them, I discovered that they were delicious, really tasty. The flavor is not oniony but more like any other commonly cooked greens. When you wash the leek leaves it is important not to let them dry all the way; the moisture left on the leaves helps steam them.

SERVES 4

1 bunch leeks	1 tablespoon butter
1 tablespoon olive oil	½ teaspoon finely chopped garlic

Cut off the white part of the leeks and save for another use. Wash the leaves and drain them. They do not have to be completely dry. Cut away about 2 inches of the tops and the bright green part at the bottom. Slice what is left into ½-inch pieces. You should have about 4 cups.

Put the olive oil, butter, and garlic in a heavy saucepan, and heat it until hot but not sizzling. Add the leek leaves and cover the pan. Lower the heat to medium and steam the leaves for 15 to 20 minutes. Serve the leek leaves as a green with meat or chicken.

SAUTÉED WILD MUSHROOMS

I like to experiment with all the wild mushrooms in the markets these days, although not all have good flavor. My favorites are morels, shiitake, and field cèpes. Oyster mushrooms are soft and delicate and I simply sauté them very gently and serve them with something light, such as chicken or veal or a steamed vegetable platter. I have about given up using cultivated mushrooms. Even one or two wild mushrooms add more flavor than a half pound of cultivated. I like to prepare morels and shiitake this way, with garlic and lemon, butter, and black pepper.

SERVES 2, OR 4 AS A GARNISH

1½ pounds morels or shiitake
    mushrooms

3 tablespoons unsalted butter

¼ teaspoon scraped garlic

½ teaspoon freshly ground black
    pepper

⅓ lemon

*Enamel or stainless steel skillet in which to
    cook the mushrooms*

Prepare the mushrooms by brushing them and looking carefully to see that no dust, ants, or other insects are on them. Cut away any decayed parts as well as the bottom part of the stem. It is better to cut the mushrooms into two pieces to prevent too much loss of juice. Heat a 9-inch skillet until hot, then drop in the butter. When the foaming stage is reached, add the mushrooms and garlic. Cook briskly over medium-high heat for 5 minutes, watching carefully not to burn them. Sprinkle the pepper in and squeeze lemon juice over the pan. Cook a few minutes more and serve as a garnish for sautéed chicken or veal.

Pumpkin with Sautéed Onions and Herbs

Pumpkin is a rich-bodied vegetable with a robust flavor that calls for strong seasonings, such as onions, garlic, and bacon. When I was young, we never thought of pumpkin as anything but another fall vegetable for cooking. We never made pumpkin pie or carved faces in pumpkins for jack-o'-lanterns. Pumpkins were planted at the end of the corn rows and when fall came and the corn was cut, the bright orange pumpkins were a sight lying in the brown fields.

SERVES 4

4 cups pumpkin flesh, peeled and cut
    into small pieces
2½ teaspoons salt
2 slices bacon
2 teaspoons butter
1 cup chopped onions

1 teaspoon dried thyme leaves
½ teaspoon freshly ground black
    pepper
1 small clove garlic
1 tablespoon finely chopped parsley

Put the pumpkin in water to cover, bring to a lively boil, and add 2 teaspoons of salt. Fry the bacon until crisp, and drain. Pour all the bacon fat from the frying pan and melt the butter in the hot pan. Add the onions, thyme, pepper, and ½ teaspoon of salt. Sauté over medium heat for 2 to 3 minutes. Scrape the peeled garlic clove to pulp and add to the pan.

Test the pumpkin after 15 minutes, when it is about half done. Drain the water off and add the onion mixture to the pan. Cover, and cook over low heat for about 15 minutes more, until done. Do not stir or you will break up the pumpkin. When ready to serve, crumble the bacon and sprinkle it and the parsley over the pumpkin.

BAKED SWEET POTATOES WITH LEMON FLAVORING

What few people today seem to realize is that there is a real difference between sweet potatoes and the tubers called yams. Yams have very moist, dark orange flesh and their skin ranges in color from almost purple to copper. Sweet potatoes have drier, cream-colored flesh and skin. It used to be that they were as plentiful in fall markets as yams, but today they're hard to find. I prefer them for cooking in syrup and roasting and always keep an eye out for them in the late autumn. Both sweet potatoes and yams are better bought in season before they are put in cold storage. Never refrigerate them or their flavor will be off, and when you get them home, leave them in a cool spot in the kitchen for several days to dry and cure before cooking.

SERVES 4

3 medium sweet potatoes (about 2½ pounds)

1 cup sugar

1½ cups water

½ teaspoon freshly grated nutmeg

3-inch strip lemon rind

¼ teaspoon salt

3 tablespoons unsalted butter

2 tablespoons lemon juice

Rinse the potatoes under warm running water. Put them in a large pot filled with boiling water and simmer briskly for about 30 minutes, until the potatoes are tender but not soft. Drain the potatoes and let them cool.

Heat the sugar, water, nutmeg, lemon rind, and salt in a large enamel or flameproof glass saucepan. Bring to a simmer and cook for 10 minutes. Add the butter and stir well. When the butter has melted, stir in the lemon juice. Remove from the heat but keep the syrup warm.

Peel the sweet potatoes and slice them into thick pieces. Butter a shallow baking dish and lay the pieces in a single layer in the dish. Stir the syrup and pour it over the potatoes. Bake them in a preheated 425°F oven for 30 minutes until bubbling hot.

Beef Barley Stew

When I was a child we would often have beef barley stew in the late fall after a steer had been butchered. It was always hung in the hide so that meat could be carved from it when needed. The stew was a nice dark brown with lots of pieces of beef and barley in it. Barley, a dried grain, is sold in health-food stores as well as supermarkets. I also like to add sautéed wild mushrooms to plain beef broth for a flavorful and simple garnish.

I find that today beef has to be treated a little specially to bring out its flavor, and, even so, it does not have as much taste as it once did. Roasting the meat and bones in the oven seems to be the best way to get good taste, and I cook the entire stew in the oven. Since chuck bones seem to have the best flavor, I ask the butcher to save them for me until he has a few pounds and then I freeze them to use as I need. I think it is a good idea to look for carefully raised beef. Some butchers and specialty shops and even farmers' markets carry organically raised beef as well as pork and chickens in limited quantities. It is more worthwhile to seek out such meats than to spend a lot of time preparing a dish that will taste disappointing.

SERVES 4

4 pounds chuck bones	3 quarts cold water
2 pounds lean beef cubes	1 tablespoon chopped parsley
1 medium onion, sliced	1 teaspoon freshly ground black pepper
1 teaspoon dried thyme leaves	⅔ cup uncooked whole-grain barley
1 bay leaf, broken into pieces	Salt

Wash the bones and meat and pat dry with cloth. Heat a heavy skillet and brown the meat on all sides. Set the browned meat aside. Put the bones in a large shallow roasting pan with the onion, thyme, and bay leaf. Add 1 quart of water and set in a preheated 350°F oven for 1½ hours to brown, turning occasionally.

Heat the remaining 2 quarts of water until just hot. Add with the parsley, cubed beef, and pepper to the roasting pan, stir well, return the pan to the oven, and reduce the heat to 300°F. Cook for about 2 hours, until the meat is tender. Remove the pan from the oven and strain the broth, discarding the

(recipe continues)

bones and onion but saving the meat. Add the barley to the broth and continue to cook in the 300°F oven for an hour, until the barley is tender. Season with salt and more pepper, if needed, and add the pieces of meat to the soup a few minutes before taking the pan from the oven.

BEEF SOUP WITH WILD MUSHROOMS

After straining the broth, remove the meat. Slice 7 to 8 wild mushrooms, such as shiitake or morels, and lightly sauté them in about 1 tablespoon of butter. Stir 1 tablespoon of sherry into the beef broth as you reheat it. Garnish each soup bowl with 6 to 8 slices of sautéed mushroom and a tablespoon or so of peeled, seeded, and cubed tomato. You may add the meat to the soup or not, as you desire.

BLACK-EYED PEAS AND
OTHER DRIED BEANS

In Virginia where I come from, black-eyed peas were the most popular dried beans we used. Farmers used to plant them to supply nitrogen to the soil, and so before the plants were chopped into the fields, anyone could go out and pick the peas, either fresh and green or when they had dried on the vine in the pods. Because they were so plentiful along the fields, no one had to grow them in the garden. (Now, however, we always plant a few rows.) We would store the dried pods in cotton sacks and then, on a cold winter afternoon when there was nothing better to do, we would shell the peas. First we would beat the sack on a table or the floor to break up the pods. You have to store black-eyed peas and all dried beans in a cold place to keep out bugs, although today a lot of beans are processed under high pressure and are less likely to be infested.

Recently, when I lived in Charleston, South Carolina, I discovered all sorts of dried beans, all different sizes and shapes and colors. There is a dish that originated in Charleston called Hoppin' John, which we had never heard of in Virginia. Supposedly, Hoppin' John was a cripple who peddled beans in the streets of Charleston and so a local dish made from red beans and rice was named for him. Red beans hold up to the long cooking necessary for this and other bean dishes; black-eyed peas just fall apart, which may explain why in Virginia we did not make many of the dishes associated with dried beans.

In coastal cities such as Charleston and Savannah and places in Louisiana, dried beans of every description are commonly cooked, probably because they were originally brought to these cities with the Africans, who used them in everyday cooking. In Africa, bean dishes are also made for feast days and other special occasions and frequently were offered to the various gods. I think this tradition is reflected here when we prepare black-eyed peas and dishes such as Hoppin' John on New Year's Day for good luck.

Black-eyed Peas in Tomato and Onion Sauce

A few years ago I decided to try cooking black-eyed peas this way instead of with a piece of pork, as everyone else does. I think the tomatoes and onions, garlic and parsley and olive oil give the peas a real interesting flavor—which, after all, they need. Black-eyed peas are a little dull, as are all dried beans.

SERVES 4

1 cup black-eyed peas

4 cups cold water

½ cup high-quality light olive oil

One medium onion (about 6 ounces), chopped

½ teaspoon crushed garlic

1¾ cups tomatoes, peeled, seeded, and cut into pieces

Salt and pepper to taste

2 tablespoons finely chopped parsley

To prepare, pick over the peas, removing the discolored ones or stones that are often found. Wash in cold water and then place in a large pot with the water. (The peas will expand and cook more uniformly if they are not crowded in the pot.) Cook over medium-high heat for 30 minutes, then test the peas. If they are tender but still firm and have no raw taste, drain them and immediately run cold water over to stop the cooking and keep them from falling apart. Drain and set aside until needed. (If they are not quite ready, cook them for another 10 minutes and test them again. Depending on how dried out they are, black-eyed peas cook at different rates. Do not overcook them—they will cook a bit more once they are in the sauce. They should be served whole in the sauce and not mushy.)

Heat a 9-inch skillet until hot, then add the olive oil. Add the onion, sauté a minute, then add the garlic and the prepared tomatoes, and cook the mixture slowly for 30 minutes. Stir often during cooking. Add the black-eyed peas, mix well, and season with salt and pepper—the peas should be well seasoned. Cook gently for 10 minutes more, then add the parsley. Spoon the beans into a casserole and set in a warm place until ready to serve. The dish can be reheated in the oven. Serve hot but not overcooked.

Thirteen-Bean Soup

It seems that there are often thirteen different kinds of beans in a packaged mixture of dried beans. I add a cup of black beans, which may bring the number of beans used up to fourteen, but it really does not matter. You could make this same soup with six kinds of beans, or three kinds, or eight. I think it is the pork that makes the soup so flavorful. Further south than Virginia, which is my home, pork is cured in salt and nitrites and then dried. In Virginia and Kentucky, where it gets colder, the pork is smoked. The pork we use has a streak of lean, too (see page 124), while in the Deep South it generally does not. For this recipe, you can use smoked bacon or another kind of smoked pork, or, if necessary, streak-of-lean in brine. I would not use fatback; it has no lean. Serve with Benne Seed Biscuits (see page 209) or yeast bread.

SERVES 4

½ cup black beans

2 cups mixed beans

1 pound smoked pork shoulder or
    streak-of-lean

1 medium onion

3 quarts cold water

1 teaspoon dried thyme leaves

1 bay leaf

Freshly ground black pepper to taste

Salt to taste

1 cup peeled, seeded, and chopped
    tomatoes

½ cup olive oil

¼ cup good sherry

Wash the beans and pick them over, casting out any stones or bad beans. Put the pork, onion, and beans in a large pot. Add the cold water, thyme, bay leaf, and pepper. Set the pot over medium-high heat and bring to a lively simmer. Turn down the heat and keep the soup at a low simmer for 2½ hours. Remove the beans from the heat when done and let them cool. Reserve the liquid. When the beans are lukewarm, season them with salt and more pepper if needed. Add the tomatoes and olive oil, and blend the mixture briefly in a blender until just smooth, but not liquefied. Add the liquid to the puréed beans, and taste for seasoning. You may not need all the liquid. Stir in the sherry and reheat until hot.

White Beans and Lentils in Tomato Sauce

When I make this dish, I cook the white beans first and then add just enough lentils for pretty color. The preparation is similar to the one I use for black-eyed peas, but the white beans have a different flavor.

SERVES 6

2 cups mixed white beans

3 pounds tomatoes, peeled and
 seeded

1 medium onion (about 6 ounces),
 peeled and coarsely chopped

⅔ cup olive oil

2 teaspoons finely crushed garlic

½ cup green lentils

2 teaspoons salt

1 teaspoon freshly ground black
 pepper

½ teaspoon cayenne

5 or 6 large basil leaves

2 tablespoons chopped parsley

Sift through the beans and discard any stones or shriveled beans. Put the beans in a 5-quart pot and add 10 cups of cold water. Bring to a boil and cook briskly until the beans are tender but not quite finished cooking—at least 1 hour. Drain and leave covered until ready to mix with the sauce. Put the tomatoes in the blender or food processor a few at a time. Process just to crush them and then remove from the blender. Do not liquefy them. Put the onion in the blender or food processor and treat it in the same way.

Heat a heavy skillet or pot until fairly hot. Add the olive oil and the onion and cook for 4 to 5 minutes. Add the garlic and tomatoes, stir well, and simmer the mixture for about 25 minutes. Meanwhile, cook the green lentils in water to cover for about 20 minutes, until not quite done, then drain them. When the tomato mixture is ready, season with the salt, pepper, cayenne, and basil. Combine the beans, lentils, and tomato mixture and cook them together until the beans are just done, about 10 minutes. Remove the basil leaves (otherwise they become too bitter), mix in the parsley, and serve hot. This dish could be served with a salad and crusty bread, or with meat.

Cabbage and Sauerkraut

No garden in Freetown, where I grew up, was complete without cabbage. Mother planted early cabbage seeds in containers in February and set them in a sunny window. She sprinkled them with a little water, covered them with burlap, and then left them for a few days. When we lifted up the burlap, there were lots of sprouts popping through the soil, which we again sprinkled with water. We would tend the cabbage plants until a warm day in March when we would plant them in the garden. These cabbages reached maturity just about the time of the spring wheat threshing and were used to feed the large group of men who arrived to help with the job. We boiled up lots of cabbage and new white potatoes for the workers and then set about planting more cabbage for the fall harvest.

Much of the fall cabbage crop was made into sauerkraut. We would put the heads of cabbage in a large wooden tub and use a huge pestle to pound them to bits. The pestle was fashioned from white oak with a big blunt piece of wood attached to the end. When enough cabbage was pounded, it was layered in a wooden barrel, alternating with good sprinklings of salt, until the barrel was full. A clean board was set over the top of the cabbage and weighted down with a great stone. The barrel was loosely covered with a clean cloth and then the cabbage was left to ferment, giving off a sour aroma all fall. The sauerkraut was ripe in time for hog butchering in the late fall and was served with fresh pork such as spareribs, pork chops, and homemade sausage.

STEWED SAUERKRAUT

Serve this sauerkraut side dish with pork chops, spareribs, or loin of pork.

SERVES 4

4 cups sauerkraut

1 pound streak-of-lean (see page 124)

1 small onion, finely chopped

3 juniper berries, or 1 teaspoon caraway
   seeds

½ teaspoon finely ground black pepper

3 cups cold water

Salt, if needed

Rinse the sauerkraut in cold running water. Drain well and rinse again. Drain and press out the excess water. Put the sauerkraut in a large saucepan and add the streak-of-lean, onion, juniper berries or caraway seeds, pepper, and water. Bring to a simmer, cover, and cook for 1½ hours, or until the sauerkraut is tender. Taste and season with salt, if necessary.

RED RICE

When I was living in Charleston a few years ago, I ate a local dish called Red Rice, a delicious mixture of rice, tomatoes, peppers, and meat or fish. What I found most interesting about it was how similar it is to a dish I had eaten with Nigerian friends. In Africa it is called Jolof rice, after the Jolof people of Gambia, and it is more of a stew, containing a leafy vegetable and usually crayfish, rather than ham. I met and talked with some elderly women in Charleston who had long ago worked in the rice fields that used to surround the city and, not surprisingly, learned that Red Rice is a very old dish. It has existed since the days of slavery, which probably explains the African connection. Once called "Charleston gold," rice is no longer cultivated in the area, although it was the first place in which rice was grown in this country and evidently the cultivation conditions are ideal. The story goes that a British ship carrying rice from Madagascar to Europe foundered off the South Carolina coast and sought refuge in the port of Charleston. The captain of the ship made the acquaintance of a local citizen and, before he set sail again, gave his new friend a little of his cargo. This small amount of rice, less than a bushel, was the beginning of the rice industry in North America.

The way I prepare Red Rice is a blending of the Charleston and African dishes, and I usually serve it as a main dish with a green salad and bread. Although about a cup will do, add as much ham or cooked fish as you have on hand—which will make the dish as substantial as you want it to be. I like to use popcorn rice, which is a recently developed variety of rice from Louisiana and tastes more flavorful than Carolina rice. Some people think it tastes like popcorn. I'm not sure it does, although it has a lovely flavor—and it does not pop.

SERVES 4

5 or 6 slices good-flavored bacon, cut into ½-inch pieces
⅔ cup chopped onions
1 teaspoon dried thyme leaves
1 green pepper, seeded and chopped
2 small, round hot peppers, seeded and chopped
2 cups fresh tomato purée
1 tablespoon brown sugar
2 cups cold water
2 cups popcorn or Carolina rice (see above)
1 cup or more small pieces cooked ham or fish
Salt and freshly ground black pepper

Cook the bacon in a heavy-bottomed saucepan until crisp. Remove the bacon pieces from the pan and set aside. Pour off half the bacon fat and heat the remaining fat over medium-high heat. Add the onions, stir, and simmer for a few minutes. Stir in the thyme and then add the green and hot peppers. Mix well and add the tomato purée and brown sugar. Add the water and stir in the rice.

Preheat the oven to 350°F.

Cover the pan and let the mixture simmer on a low burner for about 15 minutes, until the rice begins to cook. Add the bacon pieces and the ham or fish, and season with salt and pepper to taste. Stir well and spoon the mixture into a casserole or rice steamer. Cover tightly and bake in the oven for 45 to 60 minutes, until the rice is tender. Keep warm until ready to serve.

Coconut Rice

This is a flavorful dish that I have enjoyed with Nigerian friends. You will need a coconut grater, which is easy to find in cookware stores, or you can use a regular four-sided grater. A lot of time can be saved if you break the coconut in half and hold the pieces against the hand-cranked coconut grater. For variety, add some diced cooked chicken or meat to the rice before putting it in the oven.

SERVES 4

1 fresh coconut, grated
3 cups water
1½ cups popcorn or Carolina rice (see previous page)
½ cup finely chopped onion
⅔ cup peeled, seeded, and chopped fresh tomato
1 teaspoon salt
Cayenne

Put the grated coconut in a bowl. Boil the water and pour it over the coconut. Let this steep for 15 minutes.

Lift the coconut meat from the bowl with a spoon and put it in a sieve or potato ricer. Press the coconut meat to extract the liquid. You should get about 2 cups. Put the coconut milk in a heavy-bottomed pot or casserole and bring to a simmer. Add the rice, onion, tomato, salt, and a good sprinkle of cayenne. Cover well and place in a preheated 350°F oven. Cook for about 1 hour, until the liquid has been absorbed and the rice is tender. Taste for seasoning and serve hot.

Sautéed Bananas

Sautéed bananas are so simple to make and are delicious with cold sliced ham, fried chicken, and roast loin of pork.

SERVES 3 OR 4

3 tablespoons butter

3 whole bananas, peeled and sliced in
   half lengthwise

Lemon juice

Heat the butter in a heavy skillet until foaming. Add the bananas, cut side down, and cook for about 2 minutes until they are golden brown. Turn them over and brown the other side. Squeeze a few drops of lemon juice over the bananas and serve hot.

BRAISED CHESTNUTS FOR STUFFING
OR SERVING WITH VEGETABLES

Chestnuts are wonderful in stuffings for turkeys and chickens and take only minutes to prepare before they are added to the rest of the stuffing ingredients. They also make a nice change when they're puréed with a little cream and served in place of rice or mashed potatoes. Once peeled, chestnuts may be frozen until needed. Wrap them loosely in parchment and foil and let them defrost at room temperature before cooking.

SERVES 4

1 pound large chestnuts   1 tablespoon butter

Prepare and peel the chestnuts as described on page 278. When the chestnuts are peeled, heat the butter in a large skillet and sauté the whole chestnuts until lightly browned. Remove the pan from the burner and set aside until you are ready to use them in stuffing or with other vegetables.

PURÉE OF CHESTNUTS

To make a purée of chestnuts, prepare and peel 1 pound of chestnuts as described on page 278. While the chestnuts are still hot, put them in a food processor or food mill with ½ cup of heated half-and-half. Add more cream if needed for a smooth texture. Blend well and keep the purée warm until ready to serve. A pound of puréed chestnuts serves 4.

Two

FROM
THE
FARMYARD

Eggs

Poached Eggs on Sliced Country Ham

Boiling an Egg

Boiled Eggs on a Bed of Wild Mushrooms in Pastry Shells

Cheese Custard

Cheese Soufflé

Head Cheese or Souse

Chicken Stock

Chicken Soup with Vegetables

Chicken Soup with Dumplings

Roast Chicken

Roast Chicken with Stuffing

Storing Food in the Refrigerator

Sautéed Chicken with Hominy Casserole

Breast of Chicken in Parchment

Sautéed Breast of Chicken

Roast Stuffed Turkey

Roast Wild Turkey

Guinea Fowl in a Clay Pot

Roast Stuffed Guinea Fowl

Brunswick Stew

Roast Pheasant (Cold or Hot) with Currant or Gooseberry Sauce

Fresh Currant Sauce

Gooseberry Sauce

Roast Stuffed Pheasant

Panfried Quail with Country Ham

Buying Duck

Roast Peking Duck with Brandied Orange Sauce

Roast Stuffed Duck

Roast Boneless Leg of Lamb

Sautéed Veal Kidneys

Rib Pork Chops with Sauterne or Madeira Wine

Pan-Braised Spareribs

Boneless Pork Roast Cooked on Top of the Stove

Crown Roast of Pork with Herb Dressing, Garnished
with Pineapple

Roast Stuffed Suckling Pig

Pork Liver Pâté

Boiled Virginia Ham

Virginia Ham

Mustard with Brown Sugar

Slice of Country Ham Baked with Pineapple

Streak-of-Lean, Salt Pork, and Bacon

Pork Sausage

Sausage Baked in Pastry with Vegetables

Sauerkraut with Pork Sausage and Whipped Potatoes

Rabbit

Rabbit Pâté

Fried Rabbit

Braised Rabbit

Stuffed Rabbit

Beef Tenderloin with Béarnaise Sauce

WHEN I WAS A CHILD, nearly every country farmyard in Virginia had a few handsome Gurnsey or Jersey cows and a flock of barred rock or Rhode Island red hens. The cows gave sweet milk and thick, rich cream; the hens fresh brown eggs. We spooned the cream over cereal and puddings and churned the rest to make golden butter. Blending the eggs, cream, butter, or milk produced cakes, pies, custards, batter breads, and ice creams that tasted far better than any you can buy today. We did not make our own cheese but we bought the most wonderful-tasting hunks of cheese from the general store for tasty custards and for eating plain. I think the cheese tasted so good because of the tender grass in the fields where the dairy cows grazed. Fortunately, you can buy good "store" cheese—or cheddar cheese—these days from Vermont, New York State, and other areas where there are small producers, just as you can, with more and more frequency, buy farm-fresh or "country" eggs.

We ate mostly pork and chicken when I was a girl. We raised some sheep for the wool but because no one had the heart to kill the sweet spring lambs, it wasn't until I was an adult that I learned to appreciate the flavor of lamb (although I ate my share of mutton when I was young). My brothers, who were skilled at hunting and trapping, brought home game birds, squirrels, and rabbits, which also were common fare on the dinner table. Southerners have never eaten much beef and our family was no exception. I rarely eat it now, either (although I do love beef tenderloin with béarnaise sauce). I feel buying beef is a hit-or-miss proposition—you can never be sure it will have much taste.

Large pieces of beef, such as the roasts and steaks so many Americans are used to, were not essential to our meals. But we did have lots of pork, game, and chicken. Fresh bacon, smoked shoulder, or streak-of-lean was used a lot in the seasoning of most dishes—without it the food was not as flavorful. I still use pork shoulder, country ham, bacon, and streak-of-lean to flavor many dishes, from greens to cheese custard. It adds such wonderful flavor but very little of the fat or calories so many people worry about these days. I do not suggest using fatback—it's nothing more than a chunk of salty fat that adds very little flavor to anything. (See page 124 for more on salt pork and streak-of-lean.)

On the farm, meats, just as vegetables, were eaten in season. Chickens were eaten all year, usually killed and cooked on the same day. Pork was slaughtered in the winter, eaten fresh soon after, and then preserved to use the rest of the year. No one would have dreamed of killing a pig in the summer except for a barbecue. Game birds were eaten in the autumn and winter; rabbits and squirrels all year round. Because we had no electricity, fresh meat was not refrigerated, but we could store it and other perishables for a few days in the spring box, even during the hottest weeks of the summer. The spring box was a covered wooden box set over the run-off stream from the spring. It had holes in both ends so that a tiny trickle of cold, clear spring water passed through it and kept any food stored inside perfectly cool. For some reason, a small gray lizard of some sort always lived nearby, a creature we called the "spring keeper." (A few years ago I met some ladies from another part of Virginia who told me they, too, called the lizard that lived by their spring box the spring keeper.) My aunt, who had a well for water rather than a spring, would put food in the bucket and keep it cold by lowering it down the well.

Pork was our mainstay. We butchered hogs early in the winter when it was cold enough to hang the freshly killed animals for a few days without spoiling. This was the only season of the year that we ate fresh pork—the spareribs, chops, and organ meats that could not be salted, put in brine, or smoked. I feel pork is about the only meat that has kept its taste over the years. We don't preserve our meat in Freetown any longer and I now buy country hams from Smithfield, Virginia (Gwaltney is my favorite smokehouse); the hams I get taste just about the way I remember them tasting. I wouldn't feel my kitchen was well stocked if I did not have a ham on hand to flavor dishes, to slice up, or to serve tucked into biscuits or perhaps with honey mustard when a friend shows up at the door, or when I am too tired to fix a bigger meal.

Preserved meats, such as Virginia ham, smoked shoulder, bacon, and sausage, have a flavor and texture all their own. They make no claims to tasting the same as fresh, and it is for this taste that I like them. I grew up with them and while we preserved them for survival (without refrigeration or a supermarket down the street we had no choice), I think their good flavor appeals to nearly everyone. I like fresh meats just as much, but I do not like frozen meat. No matter how well it is wrapped, how quickly it is frozen, and how carefully it is thawed, it never tastes as good as fresh. For one thing, as it thaws the juice runs out, and with it goes much of the flavor. I am against the habit of shopping once a week or less and stocking up on lots of meat and stowing it in the freezer. I shop every day. I like to buy fresh food and if I don't get to the market, I often miss good-tasting foods that come and go without warning. I realize it is difficult for many families to shop this often but it is well worth the effort to stop by the market two or three times a week to have fresh meat. It is also important to take the fresh meat from the plastic wrappers as soon as you get home, rewrap it in wax paper, and store it in the refrigerator until you are ready to cook it. (See box on storing food in the refrigerator, page 81.)

To get the best flavor from poultry, game birds, pork, lamb, and beef, I suggest buying them, whenever possible, from a reliable butcher or, better still, from a farmers' market, where small farmers often sell meat from animals raised on organically grown feed. Range-fed chickens and hand-raised lamb taste far better than the meat available in most supermarkets, and you really should treat yourself whenever possible. I found the best, lightest-tasting chickens recently at New York's Union Square Greenmarket—nearly as good as those I ate as a young girl. Free-ranging chickens, which have been permitted to exercise and develop some muscle, have truly dark meat near the bones and delicious flavor throughout.

Sausage is a great favorite of mine. Some that is sold in supermarkets is pretty good, but I still prefer to make it myself. For one thing, you know exactly what is going into the sausage when you mix it in your own kitchen, and with a little experimenting, you can make it just the way you like it. You also can add enough fat. Fat is important to sausage because without it, there is little flavor. Most of the fat melts out of the sausage during cooking anyway, and I feel a small piece of homemade sausage has more flavor than half a dozen links of so-called "lean" commercial sausage. Sausage is one of the few meats that I freeze, so preparing a lot at once makes good sense.

I am so glad that more and more alternatives to mass-produced meats and poultry are popping up all the time. Small farmers across the country are turning their hands to raising organically fed chickens, lamb, veal, pork, and farm-raised game birds. The trend shows, I think, that we care more than we used to about how meats taste and how they can affect our health. These meats might cost more, but as with all good-tasting things, you may not need as much—the honest flavor compensates for the quantity.

Eggs

I know there is not supposed to be any difference between white and brown eggs when it comes to baking and cooking, but I always try to use brown eggs. I feel that cakes and breads brown better when they are made with brown eggs, but I have never conducted a test to see if I am right. Brown eggs are laid by dark, heavy birds such as barred rock and Rhode Island reds. Small, lightweight white leghorns—the chicken we commonly see—lay white eggs.

What really does make one egg better than another is freshness. It is becoming more and more possible to buy fresh eggs, preferably produced from organically fed chickens, at health-food stores, greengrocers, and even some supermarkets, and I suggest doing so whenever you can. I think they just taste better than the eggs from large commercial factories. If you eat very few eggs, try to buy just a few loose eggs at a time rather than store a dozen for weeks in your refrigerator.

Country eggs do not need to be refrigerated. At home in Virginia, my sister just sets the eggs down in a cool place after she gathers them and because they are so fresh, they keep for days. Once you refrigerate eggs, you have to keep them cold or they turn watery. You should store them in the cardboard package they come in to help protect them from the air. You can tell the freshness of the eggs by the membrane attached to the inside of the shell. If the egg is fresh the membrane is puffed out, but in stale eggs the membrane is collapsed and flattened and looks thick.

POACHED EGGS ON SLICED COUNTRY HAM

Few dishes are as nice as a well-poached egg resting on a slice of Virginia ham. I like to complete the plate with some Glazed Apples (page 111) and Grits (page 39) with Shrimp Paste (page 151). As with all egg cooking, poached eggs are best if the eggs are very fresh. Poach them one at a time and serve them right away. You will have to stand in the kitchen for a few minutes while others wait at the table, but the short delay is worth it.

SERVES 4

⅓ cup cider vinegar   4 slices Virginia ham
4 fresh eggs

Fill a 2-quart saucepan with cold water and bring it to the near boil. Add the cider vinegar. Gently crack an egg and hold it above the water. Open the shell and let the egg drop in the water. The egg will plunge to the bottom of the pan and during the fall the white will begin to set and cover the egg yolk completely. When the egg is done, it will float to the top. Lift the egg out with a slotted spoon and gently blot the bottom of the spoon with a folded paper towel to absorb water from the egg. Place the egg on top of a slice of ham already set on a plate and serve at once. Continue with the rest of the eggs and ham.

BOILING AN EGG

When I hard-boil eggs, I start them in cold water and let the water come just to a low simmer. I keep the water at this simmer for 20 to 25 minutes, then take the eggs from the water. If you boil eggs too hard, the yolks can get black around the edges. Of course, it helps a lot to start with fresh eggs when you are boiling them or cooking them any other way.

BOILED EGGS ON A BED OF WILD MUSHROOMS IN PASTRY SHELLS

This is a good brunch or Sunday breakfast dish that can be made a little ahead of time and assembled just before serving.

SERVES 4

¾ pound wild mushrooms, such as shiitake or morels
6 tablespoons (¾ stick) butter
Salt
Freshly ground black pepper
6 shallots, finely chopped

4 cups heavy cream
½ teaspoon dried thyme leaves
12 hard-boiled eggs, at room temperature
4 baked pastry shells (see page 258)
¼ cup finely chopped parsley

Preheat the oven to 350°F.

Brush any grit from the mushrooms and slice them into 1 or 2 pieces, depending on their size. Heat 3 tablespoons of butter in a skillet and add the mushrooms. Cook, tossing, for about 3 minutes, until softened. Lift the mushrooms from the skillet and let them drain on paper towels or a clean cloth. Sprinkle with a little salt and pepper.

Heat 3 more tablespoons of butter in a wide skillet, and when it melts add the shallots. Sauté for several minutes, until they become soft but not brown. Add the cream and stir well. Cook over medium heat until the cream is reduced by a third, about 5 or 6 minutes. Season with about ½ teaspoon each of salt, pepper, and thyme. Taste the sauce and adjust the seasoning. Take the sauce from the heat and keep warm.

Peel and quarter the eggs. Arrange the pastry shells on an ovenproof platter or dish. Spoon an equal amount of mushrooms into each shell and then distribute the egg quarters on top of the mushrooms. Spoon the sauce over the eggs and sprinkle with parsley. Bake for 15 minutes, until hot all the way through, and serve at once.

CHEESE CUSTARD

I like to make this custard because, unlike a soufflé, it holds up for 20 minutes or so after cooking. It is a full lunch dish, especially if you add small julienne pieces of country ham, peas, or cooked crabmeat and serve with a Bibb lettuce salad and crusty homemade bread. I have made the custard with as many as three or four different cheeses—whatever I have on hand. As well as Swiss and Gruyère, I have also used cheddar and even goat cheese.

SERVES 4

1 medium Idaho potato, peeled and
   julienned (about ⅔ cup)
1 cup heavy cream (not ultra-
   pasteurized)
2 egg yolks

½ teaspoon salt
¼ teaspoon cayenne
1 cup finely grated cheese, half Gruyère
   and half Swiss or other cheese

Drop the potatoes into a saucepan of boiling water and cook for about 3 minutes, until they begin to look translucent. Drain well. They should be firm to the touch. Put the cream in a mixing bowl with the egg yolks, salt, and cayenne. Mix well but do not beat too much air into this cream mixture. Spread the grated cheese over the bottom of a 7-inch-wide and ¾-inch-deep buttered casserole dish. Place the sliced potatoes over the cheese. Pour the cream mixture over the potatoes and bake in a preheated 350°F oven for 20 to 25 minutes, until custard is set and a buttery cream color. Be careful not to overcook. Serve with a Bibb lettuce salad and crusty homemade bread.

CHEESE SOUFFLÉ

For this recipe, I combine an aged cheddar with Gruyère to balance the good cheese flavor of the soufflé, which is a nicely flavored lunch dish. It tastes deliciously of cheese, particularly if the cheddar is a good sharp one. I like to buy a very good Vermont cheddar. A soufflé is a good way to use cheese for a main course dish without meat, and almost everyone likes it. A lot of people are intimidated by the idea of making a soufflé but shouldn't be. Just try one. Follow the instructions and do not let it overcook. Whatever you do, be sure to use real cheese when you make a soufflé—never make one with processed cheese. It won't taste good.

SERVES 4

5 ounces sharp white cheddar	3 egg yolks, slightly beaten
3 ounces Gruyère	½ teaspoon salt
2 tablespoons butter	¼ teaspoon cayenne
2 tablespoons flour	1 teaspoon dry mustard
1 cup warm milk	5 egg whites

Preheat the oven to 425°F. Butter a 1½-quart soufflé dish, and set it on top of the stove or in a warm place to warm up.

Grate the cheeses using the next to the finest side of a four-sided grater. Melt the butter in a heavy saucepan over medium-high heat. Add the flour, and cook a few minutes, stirring, until the flour is well blended, without browning. Pour in the warm milk, stirring all the while. Remove the pan from the burner and add the egg yolks, mixing them in well. Add the grated cheeses and mix thoroughly. Add the salt, cayenne, and dry mustard, and mix well again. The cheese should melt in the warm sauce without further cooking on top of the stove. Cover the pan lightly and leave to cool a bit before mixing in the beaten egg whites. Beat the egg whites to soft peaks. Stir the cheese batter and pour it onto the egg whites, then fold the whites into the batter gently and thoroughly until well blended. Spoon the mixture into the soufflé dish. (Or you could use individual ramekins.) Fill the dish three-fourths full. Set the soufflé dish in the preheated oven. After 5 minutes, turn the oven down to 400°F, and cook for 15 minutes. Serve at once.

Head Cheese or Souse

At hog-butchering time in Virginia when I was young, a number of dishes were prepared from the cuts of the pig that were not put down for long curing. These included some of my favorites, such as sausage, liver pudding, and a spicy dish called souse, or head cheese. Every housewife added a different flavor to her souse, which is made from the head and feet of the hog, but it was always highly seasoned. Souse is served as a side dish or a snack and although you do not see it much today, it was very popular then. If you want to try it, ask the butcher to order a pig's head; it is easy to find pig's feet. The head will be cleaned and ready to cook.

SERVES 12 OR MORE

1 pig's head	1 teaspoon black peppercorns
3 pig's feet	Salt
2 whole carrots, peeled	1 teaspoon dried thyme leaves
1 whole large onion	Freshly ground black pepper
3 stalks celery with leaves	Cider vinegar
4 sprigs parsley	Port or sweet sherry
2 bay leaves	

Place the meat, carrots, onion, celery, parsley, bay leaves, peppercorns, 1 tablespoon salt, and thyme in a large pot and add enough water to cover everything by about 2 inches. Bring to a simmer. Cook for about 2 hours, until the meat is tender to the touch. Remove the meat from the pot. Lift out the vegetables and discard, and strain the stock through a clean, odor-free cloth.

When the meat has cooled, cut it off the bone and into small pieces. Place the pieces in a bowl. Season the stock to taste with salt and freshly ground black pepper. Add ¼ cup cider vinegar, which gives a spiced flavor. Then add 1 cup port or sweet sherry. Taste and add extra vinegar or sherry if you want to. Pour the seasoned stock over the meat. Cover, and store in the refrigerator or other cold spot until the liquid develops into a firm jelly. This should take 3 or 4 days. Slice the souse into pieces and serve with bread, crackers, or plain. Leftover souse will keep at least 1 week refrigerated.

Chicken Stock

Over the years I have found that the most flavorful chicken stock is made from chickens initially cooked without any added fat or liquid. I simply sear pieces of chicken until all their juices are extracted. At this point I add water to the stock—always bottled water because of its pure flavor. I do not believe in cooking stock for a long period of time; it loses its good taste. I also do not like stock that has boiled. There is definitely a difference in flavor between boiled chicken soup and one that has barely simmered. You can use a whole chicken for the stock or the backs, necks, and wings of several chickens. With this method, you will get about 2 cups of stock from a 3-pound chicken, and although you need a lot of chickens to get a fair amount of stock, the flavor is great. It is so intense that you can dilute the rich base with water to make soups. When I serve chicken soup with vegetables, I like to serve the vegetables separately, either very finely cut up or lightly sautéed. Cooking vegetables in stock disguises the flavor of the vegetables and changes the true flavor of the stock. This way, guests can choose which vegetables they want to add to their bowl.

MAKES ABOUT 2 CUPS

One 3-pound chicken, or 3 pounds chicken backs, necks, and wings	1 cup finely chopped onions
	3 or 4 fresh basil leaves (optional)
Salt	2 cups cold water (preferably bottled)

Cut the chicken into 1½-inch pieces. You may ask the butcher to do this for you. Rinse the chicken pieces well and dry them. Lightly sprinkle the bony parts with salt.

Set a heavy-bottomed pot over high heat and let it get very hot. Put the chicken pieces and chopped onions in the pot. They will begin to sear right away. Stir the chicken constantly for about 5 minutes. After 5 minutes or so, the aroma will change noticeably from the time the chicken first began to sear. At this point, add the basil and cover the pot tightly. (Only add basil if it is fresh; do not substitute dried basil leaves.) Turn the heat down very low and continue to cook for 15 minutes before lifting the lid and looking at the chicken.

After 15 to 20 minutes, the stock will begin to develop. When the liquid exuded from the chicken is nearly level with the chicken pieces, add the water, cover, and continue cooking over low heat for 15 minutes more.

Strain the stock through a sieve and let it cool. The chicken pieces have almost no flavor, but if you want to, you can use them for another recipe. Pour the stock into a defatting cup to separate the fat from the liquid, or skim the fat from the surface with a spoon when the stock cools. Taste the stock and add more water if it is too strong. Pour into a glass jar and cover tightly. Store in the refrigerator until ready to use, but for no longer than 4 or 5 days.

CHICKEN SOUP WITH VEGETABLES

To serve 3 or 4 people, make stock following the basic recipe but use 3 cups of water, not 2 cups. Use bottled water if possible. Heat the soup until piping hot and season it to taste with salt and freshly ground pepper. Serve it with a platter holding 1 cup of finely shredded carrot and 1 cup of Sautéed Wild Mushrooms (see page 44). You could also serve finely chopped celery or cubed boiled potatoes.

CHICKEN SOUP WITH DUMPLINGS

I like the flavor and texture of filled dumplings in chicken soup. Put the steamed dumplings in the soup bowls and then ladle the hot chicken stock over them just before serving. These dumplings are filled with a delicious mixture of chicken, chopped vegetables, and herbs. The dumpling dough is the same as the one for the Blackberry Roly-poly on page 253, without the sugar.

SERVES 4

DUMPLING DOUGH

1 cup unbleached all-purpose
   flour
¼ teaspoon salt
3 teaspoons single-acting baking
   powder (see page 208)

1 tablespoon chilled butter, cut into
   pieces
2 tablespoons chilled lard, cut into
   pieces
¼ cup milk

FILLING

1 cup finely chopped chicken,
   preferably from the thigh
¼ cup finely chopped carrot
1 tablespoon finely chopped celery
   leaves
¼ cup finely chopped onion
2 tablespoons fine bread crumbs

½ teaspoon dried thyme leaves
¼ teaspoon crumbled dried sage
   leaves
½ teaspoon salt
Freshly ground black pepper
3 tablespoons melted butter

4 cups well-flavored chicken stock (see
   page 74)

3 cups water

To make the dough, put the flour, salt, and baking powder in a large bowl and stir well. Add the butter and lard and blend with a pastry blender or your fingertips until the mixture resembles cornmeal. Add the milk and stir with a spoon until the dough is well mixed. Spoon the dough onto a lightly floured surface, dust lightly with flour, and then knead for a minute or two. Gather

1 teaspoon salt

½ teaspoon freshly ground black pepper

1 teaspoon Provence herbs (optional)

½ teaspoon dried thyme leaves

One 3-pound chicken, or 3 poussin chickens

3 tablespoons butter, softened

3 tablespoons water

Mix together thoroughly the salt, pepper, Provence herbs (if you are using them), and thyme. Wash the chicken well under cold tap water and pat it dry inside and out with paper towels or a clean dish towel. Using a spatula, butter the inside of the chicken and sprinkle half a teaspoon of the herb mixture in the cavity. Tie the legs securely to keep the chicken closed up. Rub the rest of the butter over the outside of the chicken and sprinkle the herb mixture lightly over it. Let the chicken sit at room temperature for an hour or so before cooking.

Preheat the oven to 450°F for the large chicken or to 425°F if you are cooking poussins. Place the chicken on a wire rack in a roasting pan and cook, uncovered, for 45 minutes. Remove the chicken to a warm platter. Spoon off all but 1 teaspoon of fat from the roasting pan, and add the water. Heat, scraping the bottom of the pan. Serve this pan juice with the chicken. Have the rest of the meal ready when the bird is cooked so it does not stand for more than a few minutes after it is taken from the oven.

ROAST CHICKEN WITH STUFFING

For my taste, stuffing should be light and tender, never soggy. When I prepare chicken or any other meat with stuffing, my son is especially excited and no matter how much I make, there never seems to be enough.

SERVES 4

STUFFING

9 or 10 slices firm white bread

⅓ cup finely chopped onion

½ cup finely chopped celery, stalks and leaves

1 teaspoon dried thyme leaves

1 teaspoon crumbled dried sage leaves

1 teaspoon salt

½ teaspoon freshly ground black pepper

⅓ cup melted butter

⅓ cup toasted almond halves

CHICKEN

One 3-pound chicken

2 tablespoons butter, softened

Salt and freshly ground black pepper

¼ cup water

The day before you plan to make the stuffing, trim the crusts from the bread and cut the slices into ¼-inch cubes. Put the bread to dry out in a colander until the next day. You should have about 3 cups of bread cubes.

The next day, put the bread cubes, onion, celery, herbs, salt, and pepper in a large bowl. Toss well, and then pour the melted butter over the bread mixture. Stir gently and add the almonds. Mix well.

Preheat the oven to 375°F.

Wash the chicken and pat it dry. Spoon the stuffing into the cavity of the chicken. Pin the opening closed with rounded toothpicks and tie the legs of the chicken together with kitchen twine. Then rub the chicken all over with softened butter and sprinkle lightly with salt, pepper, and thyme. Put the chicken on a rack in a shallow pan, breast side up. Roast for 1½ hours, basting every 20 minutes, until the juices run clear when the thigh is pricked. Remove the toothpicks and twine, and set the chicken on a warm platter to rest 15 minutes. Spoon off most of the fat in the roasting pan, add the water, and bring to a boil, scraping up all the browned bits. Strain and serve with the chicken.

Storing Food in the Refrigerator

The refrigerator makes food storage so much easier than it used to be, but I can't help feeling that we abuse its usefulness by refrigerating too many kinds of food. Onions, shallots, and garlic, for instance, go through a false dormant period when chilled and begin to sprout in the refrigerator and lose flavor. Fruits and berries, cakes and breads (which keep fine in a cool pantry if properly covered and wrapped) should be permitted to sit at room temperature before being eaten to give their flavors time to come out.

Milk and cream should, of course, be kept very cold. I pour milk and cream from the cardboard or plastic cartons into glass bottles; glass holds the cold much better.

As soon as I get home from the market, I unwrap fish, poultry, and meat and rewrap it in fresh wax paper and foil. I take out whatever I find in the cavity of the chicken and wipe the whole chicken with a damp cloth. I do the same for meat. I refrigerate the well-wrapped food in lidded nonaluminum metal or enamel containers, which conduct cold air well.

I think it is particularly important to remove plastic wrappings from meats, fruits, and vegetables. Plastic is about the worst conductor for cold air and foods just seem to heat up the minute they are put in plastic. I have found that fresh produce such as salad greens wilt more quickly in the plastic vegetable bins found in most new refrigerators and so I always try to replace mine with enamel or glass containers.

Sautéed Chicken with Hominy Casserole

Hominy was as common on the table when I was growing up as rice is today. It is not used too much anymore but is still readily available in some regions, particularly in the South. You can buy it in cans or loose, sold in bulk, and sometimes you can find it in health-food stores and packaged alongside the other grains in the supermarket. The brand I buy is Monte Blanco by Goya. I have found that Spanish brands are more tasty. After you have opened the can, wash the hominy 3 or more times with cold water and drain well. This removes the taste of the liquid it soaked in. Hominy is dried, hulled whole kernels of corn; grits are finely ground hominy. Usually hominy is boiled and served hot for breakfast, plain or with gravy. Because I think it is a little like tiny dumplings, I like to cook it with sautéed chicken so that the juices from the chicken and the vegetables can mingle with the hominy.

SERVES 4

One 2½-pound chicken	½ teaspoon freshly ground black
3 tablespoons butter	pepper
3 cups hominy	Pinch dried thyme leaves
1 medium onion, chopped	¼ cup white wine (not too dry)
¼ pound mushrooms, sliced	½ teaspoon salt
1 small carrot, thinly sliced	1 tablespoon finely chopped parsley
1 bay leaf	2 tablespoons heavy cream (optional)

Cut the chicken into 8 pieces. Rinse it under cold water and pat dry. Heat the butter in a skillet and when it foams, quickly sauté the chicken pieces, turning them so that they cook on both sides but do not brown. This seizes the skin so it does not shrivel during cooking. Drain the chicken on paper towels.

Put the hominy in a 2-quart casserole with a lid. Lay the chicken pieces on top and cover with an even layer of onion, sliced mushrooms, and carrot. Add the bay leaf and sprinkle the pepper and dried thyme over the vegetables. Add the wine and cover the casserole.

Cook in a preheated 325°F oven for 45 minutes. About 5 minutes before the casserole has finished cooking, add the salt and parsley. Take it from the oven and remove the bay leaf. Taste and add the cream if you want it. I do not always add it.

BREAST OF CHICKEN IN PARCHMENT

wonderful aroma explodes from the packet
. I find that chicken breasts and fish, which
perfect for parchment cooking, and I have
in Parchment with Mixed Vegetables on
r this recipe should be small and flattened
k, they will puff up during cooking. Serve
n rice.

ned	1 pound fresh carrots, julienned
	12 shiitake or other wild mushrooms, sliced
ck	¼ cup chopped parsley
;	½ cup white wine
ned	
	4 fresh tarragon leaves
	Four 18-by-15-inch sheets parchment paper

and. Start with the 4 sheets of parchment
ablespoon of butter over each sheet to coat
l be placed. Arrange 1 sliced shallot on each
ith a pinch of salt. Place a chicken breast on
alt mixture. Cover each breast with a quar-
maining shallots, and parsley, and top each
or so of butter. Too much butter will make

sides of the paper. Spoon 2 tablespoons of
ie the parchment together very securely. You

(recipe continues)

can use twine or twist ties. Set the packets on a large cookie sheet and bake for 20 minutes. Do not bake longer than this or the chicken will be overcooked. Meanwhile, make the sauce by heating the cream to a rapid boil in a wide frying pan over high heat. Cook until the cream has been reduced by about one-third, which takes only 4 or 5 minutes. Lower the heat and add the salt and sherry to taste. Stir in the cayenne and the tarragon leaves and remove the pan from the heat. Keep warm until the chicken is ready. Take the chicken from the oven and put one packet on each plate. Snip the parchment open at the table so that the aroma and taste of the dish are fully appreciated. Serve with the warm sauce.

Sautéed Breast of Chicken

Simple sautéed chicken breasts can finish cooking in a low oven. Serve them with plain rice and salad. For a lighter dish, add 2 tablespoons of cold water to the skillet rather than the heavy cream. Stir well to mix with the contents of the pan and pour this light sauce over the chicken.

SERVES 4

4 whole boned chicken breasts
1 cup flour seasoned with ½ teaspoon
    freshly ground black pepper and
    1½ teaspoons salt
4 tablespoons (½ stick) butter
½ lemon

12 mushrooms, halved
¼ teaspoon finely chopped garlic
1 cup heavy cream
5 fresh tarragon leaves
1½ tablespoons sherry

Preheat the oven to 300°F.

Cut each chicken breast in half. Pound the pieces slightly, especially the thick ends. Wash, dry, and dredge with the seasoned flour.

Heat an ovenproof skillet, then add 3 tablespoons of the butter and melt over medium-high heat. When the butter is foamy, add the chicken breasts and cook for 2 to 3 minutes, until the meat is seared but not browned. Turn the meat and squeeze a little lemon juice on each piece. Cover the skillet and set it in the oven for about 15 minutes.

Melt the remaining tablespoon of butter in another skillet and add the mushrooms and garlic. Sauté for a few minutes, take from the heat, and set aside.

Arrange the chicken on a heated platter. Spoon out most of the fat and then add the heavy cream to the skillet. Bring the cream to a boil over medium-high heat and reduce it until it is thickened. Add the tarragon and sherry, remove from the heat, and stir. Spoon the cream sauce over the chicken and garnish with the mushrooms.

Roast Stuffed Turkey

This old-fashioned turkey stuffing is easy to make and stays nice and moist inside the roasting turkey. There is nothing fancy about the recipe—it is a good, plain traditional stuffing, to which, if you want to, you can add sausages or chestnuts. There is no reason to buy a frozen turkey. It doesn't taste as good as fresh, and the fresh are easily available today.

SERVES 10 TO 12

STUFFING

2 loaves unsliced white bread, crusts removed	2 teaspoons freshly ground black pepper
3 cups chopped onions (about ¼-inch cubes)	2 teaspoons dried thyme leaves
1½ cups chopped celery	1 tablespoon crumbled dried sage leaves
3 tablespoons chopped celery leaves	2 teaspoons Bell Seasoning
2 teaspoons salt	1½ cups melted butter

TURKEY

One 12- to 15-pound turkey	½ cup melted butter

GRAVY

⅓ cup flour	Water
Pan drippings	Salt and freshly ground black pepper

The day before you plan to make the stuffing, set the bread out on the counter. The next day, cut the day-old bread into ¼-inch cubes—you should have about 12 cups of bread cubes. Mix together the bread cubes, onions, celery, celery leaves, salt, pepper, thyme, sage, and Bell Seasoning. Pour the butter into the bowl and toss well to mix.

Preheat the oven to 425°F.

Spoon the stuffing into the turkey. Pin the opening with toothpicks or skewers. Tie the legs together with kitchen twine and tuck the wings under the body. Put the turkey on a rack in a roasting pan, breast side up, and brush it with melted butter. Set the pan in the oven, and roast the turkey for 45 minutes. Reduce the temperature to 350°F, and cook for 2¼ hours longer, basting every 20 minutes.

Remove the turkey to a platter and let it rest for 20 minutes before carving. Meanwhile, make the gravy with the pan drippings. Scrape the bottom of the pan to loosen any browned bits and then pour the drippings into a glass measuring cup and let the fat rise to the surface. Skim off about ½ cup of fat and put it in a large skillet. Discard the rest of the fat but save the drippings. Add the flour and blend it into the fat over medium-high heat until smooth. When the flour browns, gradually add the rest of the drippings, scraping up all the browned bits. Stirring all the while, add enough water for the right consistency for gravy, and simmer until thickened. Strain the gravy into the top of a double boiler and season it to taste with salt and pepper. Keep it warm over barely simmering water for at least 20 minutes, until you are ready to serve it with the turkey and stuffing. The longer it cooks in the double boiler, the better it will taste.

NOTE:

If you have leftover stuffing that will not fit inside the turkey, put it in a rice steamer and add drippings from the roasting pan—you can collect them during roasting. You will need about 4 cups of liquid, so supplement the pan drippings with water. Gently steam the stuffing for 35 minutes—it will be much more moist and flavorful than if you baked it in a casserole alongside the turkey.

ROAST WILD TURKEY

It used to be something very special if a hunter bagged a wild turkey during hunting season and shared it with neighbors and friends. But today wild turkeys can be netted and are then sold in some good butcher shops that sell game, so they are a bit more available. Wild turkey has a firm flesh and it is good to ask the butcher to let it hang in a cold spot either in the feather or plucked. When you cook this wild bird, your kitchen is filled with the most interesting aroma. The taste is deliciously turkey, the flesh a little more dense, and the wings and legs more tender than with domestic turkey. It is best to cook wild turkey in a covered pot, such as a long oval Le Creuset that has a cover, and keep the turkey at a low heat so that it doesn't dry out. Wild turkeys run smaller than domestic ones—from 6 to 10 pounds or more. A 6- to 8-pound bird will easily serve 6 to 8 persons. All of the meat is tender and delicious and there's lots of white meat. I like a simple dressing of sage and onion. The turkey juices flavor the dressing so much that I do not need the richness of sausage or the sweetness of chestnuts—I just savor the good taste of the wild turkey. Fresh Currant Sauce (see page 98) or wild lingonberry sauce, which you can get ready-made in a Scandinavian shop, is delicious served alongside.

SERVES 6 TO 8

STUFFING

4 cups white bread cut into ¼-inch cubes

1 cup finely chopped celery

1 cup finely chopped onions

2 tablespoons finely cut celery leaves

1 teaspoon salt

1½ teaspoons dried thyme leaves

2 teaspoons crumbled dried sage leaves

1 teaspoon freshly ground black pepper

⅓ cup melted butter

TURKEY

One 6- to 8-pound dressed wild turkey

⅓ cup butter, softened

1 teaspoon freshly ground black pepper

1½ teaspoons dried thyme leaves

1½ teaspoons salt

1 cup cold water

SAUCE

¼ cup or more water   Salt and pepper to taste

¼ cup flour

Put the bread cubes, celery, onions, celery leaves, salt, thyme, sage, black pepper, and melted butter in a large bowl and toss until well mixed. Rinse the turkey under cold water, then pat dry inside and out with a clean cloth. Fill the cavity with the stuffing, sew up the opening, and tie the legs in place with the wings tucked under the bird. Rub all over with some of the soft butter and sprinkle with the pepper and thyme mixed together. Set aside in the cooking pot for 1 or 2 hours in a cold spot until ready to place in the oven. Sprinkle the salt over the turkey and add 1 cup cold water to the pot. Cover, and place in a 350°F oven. Cook for 1½ hours before basting with some more soft butter, then turn the heat down to 325°F and baste every 20 minutes. After 2 hours of cooking, test for tenderness: uncover the pot and press your fingers against the turkey thigh—the flesh should give. If it does not, cover and continue to cook 45 minutes more. Test again—the flesh should be more tender and really give now. Watch carefully at this point to see that the bird does not overcook. If the leg is tender, the rest of the bird is done. Remove the turkey from the oven, uncover, and put it on a hot platter in a warm spot.

Pour the liquid from the pot into a bowl, scraping out any residue on the bottom. Set the cooking pot on a burner and add ¼ cup water to loosen the remaining brown bits, then pour into the bowl. Skim 4 tablespoons of fat from the top of the liquid in the bowl and put it in a skillet. Heat until nearly smoking, then add the flour, stirring. Cook over moderate heat, stirring, 4 to 5 minutes until the butter-flour mixture has turned a good dark brown color without burning. Pour the defatted liquid from the bowl into the skillet, stir well, and simmer for 15 minutes. While cooking, season with salt and pepper to taste and add a bit of water, if the sauce seems too thick, and skim off any fat that may gather on top. Strain the sauce and keep hot until ready to serve.

When you carve the turkey, remove the skin first (cooked this way, the skin will not have browned).

Guinea Fowl in a Clay Pot

Guinea fowl are small prehistoric-looking birds that are getting more and more popular. I believe the ones you buy today taste so good because they are being raised in captivity and growers are paying a lot of attention to feeding them well. The best place to buy them is from a reliable butcher who sells a lot of poultry, but even so you might have to order them. Guinea fowl are dry—there is nothing anyone can do about it—and so I think the best pot to cook them in is a clay pot because clay holds moisture so well. A clay pot is easy to use once you soak it. Just put the food in it, seal it with the lid, and then stop worrying about dinner until it's cooked. I cook guinea fowl with leeks, onions, mushrooms, and herbs to give them good flavor and succulence.

SERVES 3 OR 4

One 2½- to 3-pound guinea fowl
4 tablespoons butter, softened
1 teaspoon salt
½ teaspoon freshly ground black pepper
Dried thyme leaves
⅔ cup sliced onions
1 small leek

1 small bay leaf
1 thin slice or so Virginia ham (about 3 ounces)
2 tablespoons white wine
3 mushrooms, sliced
Finely chopped parsley, for garnish
Fresh Currant Sauce (see page 98)

Soak the clay pot in cold water for half an hour. Wash the guinea fowl under cold tap water. Pat dry inside and out. Paint the inside cavity with 2 tablespoons of soft butter. Make a mixture of the salt, pepper, and 1 teaspoon thyme. Sprinkle half of it into the cavity. Paint the outside of the guinea fowl with another tablespoon of butter and sprinkle over with the rest of the salt mixture.

Remove the clay pot from soaking and drain. Scatter the sliced onions in the bottom, sprinkle in a pinch of thyme, and add the leek and bay leaf. Place the guinea fowl in the pot, and lay the slice of ham over it. Cover, and set the pot in a cold oven. Turn the oven on to 350°F and cook for 45 minutes. Remove the cover and the slice of ham, turn the bird over, and place the ham back on top of it. Splash in 2 tablespoons of white wine. Cover and cook 15 minutes more, or until done, when springy to the touch of the forefinger.

In the meantime, sauté the mushrooms in the remaining tablespoon of butter for 3 minutes and scatter them into the pot just before serving. Remove the guinea fowl to a platter and serve with the sauce of onions and mushrooms poured over it and garnished with finely chopped parsley. Serve with Fresh Currant Sauce.

ROAST STUFFED GUINEA FOWL

A moist, flavorful stuffing brings out the good taste of a guinea fowl and helps the naturally dry bird taste succulent and juicy.

SERVES 4

STUFFING

6 or 7 slices firm white bread

1 large tart apple

1 tablespoon sugar

½ cup finely chopped onion

1 tablespoon celery leaves

1 teaspoon dried thyme leaves

2 teaspoons crumbled dried sage leaves

¼ teaspoon crushed garlic

1½ teaspoons salt

1 teaspoon freshly ground black pepper

⅓ cup melted butter

¼ pound sausage, cooked and crumbled

GUINEA FOWL

Two 2½-pound guinea fowl

3 tablespoons butter, softened

1 teaspoon dried thyme leaves

½ teaspoon salt

½ teaspoon freshly ground black pepper

3 to 4 tablespoons water

The day before you plan to make the stuffing, trim the crusts from the bread and cut the slices into ¼-inch cubes. Put the bread in a colander to dry out until the next day. You should have about 2 cups of bread cubes.

The next day, peel the apple and cut it into 8 slices. Lay the apple slices on a plate and sprinkle them with sugar.

Put the bread, onion, celery leaves, herbs, garlic, salt, and pepper in a large bowl, and toss well. Pour the melted butter over the mixture and stir to combine. Add the apples and sausage and toss.

Preheat the oven to 350°F.

Rinse the guinea fowl and pat them dry. Spoon the stuffing into the cavities of both, pin the openings closed with rounded toothpicks, and tie the legs closed with kitchen twine. Rub them with softened butter. Mix together the thyme, salt, and pepper and sprinkle the mixture over the guinea fowl. Put them in a deep enamel pot, cover, and roast for 1½ hours, basting every 15 to

20 minutes. Press the skin with your fingertips and if it feels springy, the birds are done.

Lift the guinea fowl from the pot and put them on a platter. Pour off the fat and set the pot on top of the stove. Add 3 to 4 tablespoons of water to the pot and cook, over high heat, scraping the brown bits from the bottom. Let the sauce boil for a few seconds, strain, and taste for seasonings. Pass the sauce separately with the guinea fowl.

BRUNSWICK STEW

If I can get either rabbit or squirrel, I like to make Brunswick stew. When I was young, there were squirrels all over the place, usually raiding the corn field. I don't think you see as many of them today because there are not as many farmers who have small corn fields surrounded by woodlands. Whenever we went to pick corn, my brother always took along his rifle so that he could get a few squirrels that were scampering in the fields. We would stew them plain or make Brunswick stew. Squirrels taste sweeter than rabbits because of the nuts they eat.

When we used to make Brunswick stew I don't remember using as many vegetables as I do now and certainly never lima beans. But the vegetables add good flavor and make the stew so filling you do not need anything else. Like other stews, this one gets better every day you warm it up, and I have included it here because it is so good, so easy to make, and is delicious as a leftover. If you prefer to make it with chicken only, increase the chicken to 5 or 6 pounds.

1 or 2 squirrels (if available), or 1 rabbit or wild hare

One 3- to 4-pound chicken (if not using squirrel or rabbit, double the amount of chicken)

1 pound smoked pork shoulder, in 1 piece

1 large onion (about 6 ounces), sliced

1 teaspoon dried thyme leaves

2½ to 3 quarts spring or bottled water

2 pounds tomatoes, peeled, seeded, and chopped

2 cups fresh lima beans

3 cups peeled and cubed potatoes

1 teaspoon freshly ground black pepper

3 cups fresh corn cut from the cob

Salt

½ cup (1 stick) butter

3 tablespoons finely chopped parsley

Wash the squirrels or the rabbit under cold running water, pat dry, and cut into about 6 pieces each. Wash and dry the chicken and cut it into 12 pieces. Wash the pieces again, drain, and set aside. Leave the smoked pork in 1 piece because it usually holds together and is easier to remove at the end of the cooking.

Put the meat in an 8- to 10-quart pot with the onion and thyme. Cover with 2½ quarts of spring or bottled water and bring to a simmer. Do not let the liquid boil as it will spoil the flavor of the stew. Simmer the stew for 2½ hours. Add the chopped tomatoes, lima beans, potatoes, and black pepper. Cover, and simmer gently for about 30 minutes. Add the corn and salt to taste, and cook for 15 minutes more, or until the lima beans are tender. Stir occasionally during the cooking to prevent sticking. If the stew becomes too thick, add 2 cups of heated bottled water. When ready to serve, swirl in the butter and parsley.

Roast Pheasant (Cold or Hot) with Currant or Gooseberry Sauce

Pheasants are testy birds to cook. They need a lot of fat on them for flavor and moistness, so you should buy only plump ones. A nice plump pheasant has a surprising amount of white meat. As with most game birds, fresh-killed pheasant, such as the kind you might buy from a pheasant farm, should be hung in a cool place for a few days to age, which brings out the flavor. I prefer to leave the feathers on the bird while it ages. Pheasant are not as dry as guinea fowl but should be cooked in a deep pan so that any liquid in the recipe has plenty of room to surround the bird during cooking. I prefer eating pheasant cold. I let it cool in a cool place in the kitchen and then refrigerate it overnight. This way it is easy to carve and the flavor is better.

SERVES 3 OR 4

One 2- to 3-pound pheasant
1 teaspoon salt
½ teaspoon freshly ground black pepper
1 teaspoon dried thyme leaves
½ cup (1 stick) butter, softened
Watercress, for garnish
Fresh Currant Sauce or Gooseberry Sauce
    (see page 99)

Preheat the oven to 375°F.

Carefully wash the outside of the pheasant and pat it dry. If the butcher has not taken the entrails from the cavity, remove them and wipe the cavity with a clean, damp cloth. Do not rinse the inside; washing takes away the special flavor characteristics of game birds.

Combine the salt, pepper, and thyme, crushing the thyme with your fingertips. Paint the inside of the bird with some of the softened butter and sprinkle with some of the seasonings. Tie the legs together with a clean white cloth or strong twine. Rub the outside with the rest of the butter and season with the rest of the salt mixture. Put the bird in a deep roasting pan with a cover. Pheasant seems to cook better in a deep pan because more moisture is kept in, which is important since pheasant can become dry during cooking. Put the covered pan in the oven and roast for 15 minutes before reducing the heat to 350°F. Cook for 1 hour 15 minutes. Test for doneness by pressing your fingers against the flesh. If it feels springy, it is done. If the bird is not cooked, the flesh will feel firm and tight.

Take the pan from the oven and remove the cover. Let it cool for a minute or two and then lift the pheasant from the pan and place it on a dish. Cover the dish and let the pheasant cool completely. Refrigerate it when it is cool. When you are ready to serve the pheasant, slice away the outer skin and then carve it as you would a roast chicken. Garnish with watercress and serve with currant jelly, Fresh Currant Sauce, or Gooseberry Sauce.

If you prefer to serve the pheasant hot, deglaze the pan with 2 tablespoons of water just after lifting the bird from the pan to the platter. Pour the liquid from the pan into a fat separator or skim off as much fat as you can with a spoon. You only need a little essence; too much water added to the pan will dilute the flavor. Pass the essence at the table.

Fresh Currant Sauce

I usually make at least two cups of currant sauce since it keeps so well in the refrigerator for a few weeks and is delicious with all kinds of game and poultry. Currants are tart berries and need sweetening, but add the sugar a little at a time and keep tasting until the sauce is right.

MAKES 2 CUPS

1 quart red currants
½ cup water

About ½ cup sugar

Rinse the currants and put them in a large, nonmetallic saucepan. Crush a few against the side of the pan with a spoon and then add the water. Cook over low heat, stirring the berries, until they begin to simmer. Add a few tablespoons of sugar and taste. Raise the heat to medium and cook the berries for 10 to 15 minutes, stirring and adding more sugar to taste. Do not let the berries scorch. When they are lightly stewed, strain the sauce through a sieve and serve the sauce warm or cold.

Gooseberry Sauce

Both green and pink gooseberries freeze well, which is fortunate since tart gooseberry sauce tastes so good with game, turkey, and other winter meats, while fresh gooseberries are available only in midsummer. We grew them when I was a child, and while not as many people seem to grow them today, I have noticed them in more and more farmers' markets every year. Freeze them as you would other berries (see page 252). Remove the stems right after you take them from the freezer. I like to cook both colors of berries and serve them in separate bowls for a pretty contrast at the table. Their flavor is the same.

1 pint fresh or frozen gooseberries   Sugar to taste
¼ cup water

Take the berries from the freezer (if they are frozen) a few hours before cooking. Remove the stems. When they are thawed, rinse them and put them in a 1-quart nonmetallic saucepan. Crush a few against the side of the pan with a spoon. Add the water and 1 rounded tablespoonful of sugar and heat on a low burner until the berries begin to cook. Raise the heat and watch the berries carefully to avoid scorching them. Cook for about 10 minutes, stirring occasionally. Strain the sauce through a sieve and serve warm or cold.

ROAST STUFFED PHEASANT

Ask the butcher to hang the pheasants for about a week before you take them home. If you ask him to clean the birds, be sure he does not wash out the cavities as this takes away some of the good gamey flavor. When you prepare the pheasants for roasting, do not rinse out the cavities, either. Nutty wild rice goes well with pheasant and the sweetness of the grapes is a pleasant contrast to their gaminess. You will need 2 cups of raw wild rice to make 4 cups cooked.

SERVES 4

4 cups cooked wild rice	2 tablespoons melted butter
1 teaspoon dried thyme leaves	Two 2½-pound well-aged pheasants
1 teaspoon salt	1 cup seedless white grapes
1 teaspoon freshly ground black pepper	

Put the wild rice in a large bowl and season it with the thyme, salt, and pepper. Toss well and then add the melted butter. Toss again.

Preheat the oven to 375°F.

Rinse the outside of the pheasants and pat them dry. Spoon the stuffing into the cavity of each bird. Roast in a shallow pan for 1 hour, then remove the birds from the oven. Poke the grapes into the stuffing, using a long-handled spoon. Return the birds to the oven and roast for 30 minutes longer. Press the birds with your fingertips; if they feel springy, they are done. Serve at once. If you want to make a little pan sauce, follow the directions for Roast Chicken (see page 80).

PANFRIED QUAIL WITH COUNTRY HAM

Quail are delightful little birds that you never have to worry about being tough. If you buy them fresh, let them age for a day or two to tenderize them. Quail are getting easier and easier to find in supermarkets and local butcher shops, and although many are sold frozen and are quite good, they are best fresh. You can also buy them from game bird farms that raise them for home buyers and restaurants. As with pheasant, I usually ask the butcher or game bird farmer to leave the feathers on the bird and the innards intact because this improves their flavor as they age. But most cooks would probably want to have the birds plucked and cleaned, which certainly is easier and does not make such a difference in flavor that I would advise against it.

I sauté quail on top of the stove in a covered pan to keep them moist, but they also do well roasted, if covered. Quail are good to make for guests because they "hold" in the pan for 15 or 20 minutes without drying out, which gives you time to get the rest of the meal organized. For this dish I call for fresh white grape juice, which adds good tart flavor. Fresh grape juice is simple to make if you have a vegetable mill or potato ricer, but do not try to make it in a blender. The blender does not extract the juice, it just purées the fruit.

SERVES 4

1 cup white grapes (to make ¼–⅓ cup grape juice)	1 teaspoon dried thyme leaves
2 teaspoons salt	8 quail, split and flattened
½ teaspoon freshly ground black pepper	½ cup (1 stick) unsalted butter
	½ pound Virginia ham, cut into 2 by ¼–inch matchsticks

First, make the fresh white grape juice. Crush the cup of grapes with a pestle, then put through a sieve or vegetable mill to extract the juice, or use a potato ricer.

Combine the salt, pepper, and thyme, crushing the thyme with your fingertips. Sprinkle both sides of the birds with the seasonings.

Melt the butter in a large skillet over medium heat until it foams and just begins to brown. Add the quail, skin side down. Sprinkle with ham, cover,

(recipe continues)

and cook for 3 to 4 minutes, until the skin is golden brown. Turn the birds and continue cooking, covered, until the juices run clear, about 4 minutes longer. Take the pan from the heat and let the quail rest, covered, for about 10 minutes. Arrange the quail on a platter and sprinkle the ham from the pan over them.

Pour the fat from the pan. Add the grape juice (you can also use water, if you prefer), and bring to a boil. Cook for 1 minute, scraping the browned bits from the bottom to deglaze the pan. Pour over the quail and serve.

BUYING DUCK

I think the best duck to buy is Peking duck. It is thinner and leaner than Long Island duck and has good flavor without the fat. You can nearly always find Peking ducks in Chinese markets, and if your city has a Chinatown, buy the ducks from a butcher shop in the area. If not, some companies mail-order Peking ducks. I buy them from California and have never been disappointed by the ducks that arrive by air freight well packed in ice. Peking ducks look different from Long Island ducks because they are longer and come with the head and feet attached. When these are cut off, the ducks weigh only about three pounds, which is a desirable size since one duck nicely serves two people.

Roast Peking Duck with Brandied Orange Sauce

What I like most about roast Peking duck is the crispy skin. To ensure this crispness, it is important to let the uncooked duck sit out in the kitchen most of the day without any covering. The air dries out the skin so that it crisps up in the hot oven. The sauce is well flavored with freshly squeezed orange juice, shallots, and brandy and tastes delicious with the moist, rich duck.

SERVES 4

Two 3-pound Peking ducks
3 oranges, halved
1 lemon, halved
2 tablespoons butter
2 tablespoons finely chopped shallots
1 tablespoon finely chopped leek
1 tablespoon grated carrot

1 tablespoon flour
1 cup fresh orange juice
1 tablespoon vinegar
2 tablespoons sugar
2 tablespoons brandy
Salt and freshly ground black pepper

The morning before you plan to cook the ducks, rinse them under cold tap water and put them on wire racks. Do not cover them but let the air of the kitchen dry them completely. They can sit out for 8 to 10 hours.

Preheat the oven to 425°F.

Put 3 orange halves and 1 lemon half inside the cavity of each duck and set them in a roasting pan fitted with a rack. Roast for 1 hour. Take the ducks from the oven but leave the oven on. Tilt the ducks over a bowl to collect the juices from the cavities. Do not let the fruit fall out. Return the ducks to the roasting pan and continue cooking for 1 hour longer. Remove the juices and pour the fat off; set the juices aside to use in the sauce.

Heat the butter in a large stainless steel frying pan. When the butter melts, add the shallots and sauté for 1 minute. Add the leek, carrot, and flour, and sauté for 4 to 5 minutes, stirring to keep the sauce smooth. Add the orange juice and vinegar and mix well. Lower the heat to a simmer.

Heat the sugar in another stainless steel pan. When it turns amber, spoon it

(recipe continues)

quickly into the rest of the sauce. It will harden at first but then will dissolve as it cooks. Pour the reserved pan juices and the brandy into the sauce and stir well. Strain the sauce and season it to taste with salt and pepper. Hold the sauce in the top of a double boiler over simmering water until you are ready to pass it with the duck. Split the ducks and remove the backbones. Serve one half per person.

SAUTÉED VEAL KIDNEYS

Most Americans are not exposed to eating kidneys and don't know how good they taste. I usually wash and soak them before I cook them, and then I slice and sauté them and serve them with a quick brandy and cream sauce—I set the brandy on fire to burn off the alcohol. These taste good with boiled potatoes or potato cakes (see page 41). I also like sautéed veal kidneys with shallot butter instead of the brandy cream sauce.

SERVES 4

3 veal kidneys

About 5 tablespoons butter

2 tablespoons brandy

3 tablespoons heavy cream

Salt and freshly ground black pepper

Lemon juice (optional)

Remove the fat from the kidneys, if necessary. There is a thin skin that usually covers the kidneys. Remove that and leave them whole. Have ready a pot of boiling water. Drop the kidneys in and remove them right away. Put them on a towel to dry while doing the next step. Heat a heavy skillet over medium heat and add 4 tablespoons of the butter. While the butter is heating, cut the kidneys into slices about ¼ inch thick. When the butter is foaming add the kidneys and the juice from the kidneys that came out while you were slicing them. Toss with a fork or a spoon for a few minutes and then pour over the brandy and set it alight. When the flames die out, add the cream and salt and pepper to taste, and cook 2 to 3 minutes more. Just before serving, drop about 1 tablespoon of butter into the pan and swirl it around. Squeeze in, if you like, a little bit of lemon juice.

Rib Pork Chops with Sauterne or Madeira Wine

These chops are from the rib or rack section of the whole pork loin. The rib and loin sections have different flavors, and since the ribs have more bone and streaks of fat, I think they have better flavor. The center-cut loin is very tender. When you buy pork, it should be light, like the color of veal, with only the slightest tinge of pink, if at all. I suggest buying it from a reliable supermarket where the turnover is apt to be high and the meat very fresh. When I lived in Virginia as a child, we always cooked pork on top of the stove and watched it carefully to be sure it was cooked through. I cook these chops in a covered pan for the same reason and to keep them from drying out. I prefer Madeira but since I do not always have it, I also use sauterne, which is not quite as sweet.

SERVES 4 OR 5

1 cup flour seasoned with salt and
    freshly ground black pepper
Five ½-inch-thick rib pork chops

3 tablespoons butter
½ cup Madeira or sauterne

Put the seasoned flour in a flat pan or dish. Take the chops and press each one in the flour, coating both sides. Shake off the excess flour and place the chops on wax paper to rest 45 minutes to 1 hour. Put the butter in a frying pan large enough to hold the chops in one layer; heat until it foams and the butter is beginning to brown lightly around the edges of the pan. Place the chops in the pan. Cook over a rather brisk heat about 5 minutes, uncovered. Cover, and cook another 10 minutes. Then remove the cover, turn the chops, and lower the heat. Cook slowly for about 10 minutes. When cooked, remove the chops from the pan to a hot platter. Pour off the fat from the pan and deglaze with the Madeira or sauterne. Stir to pick up all the browned bits coating the pan. Swirl the pan around until the sauce becomes thick and syrupy. At this point quickly pour the sauce over the chops and serve with sautéed spinach (page 18) and popcorn rice or a julienne of mixed vegetables and white potato cakes (page 41).

Pan-Braised Spareribs

When the bacon is cut from the hog, the ribs are sheared off. These ribs are too thin to smoke and should be cooked right away, fresh. The bottom four ribs are all gristle, so it is best to buy the top section of ribs, the top eight inches or so. Ask the butcher to trim away the meaty part on the bottom of the ribs, which is tough and requires more cooking time than the rest of the rib. He should also crack the ribs across the center, but not break them into two pieces. Many people do no more than marinate ribs before grilling them, but I always parboil the ribs first, in case they are tough, then I marinate, braise, or panfry them.

SERVES 4

5 pounds spareribs
1 medium to large onion

MARINADE

3 tablespoons brown sugar
¼ cup honey
⅔ cup soy sauce
6 tablespoons sweet sherry

½ cup strained chili sauce
1 tablespoon finely grated fresh
  gingerroot
3 cloves garlic, crushed

Put the ribs and the onion in a rectangular pan with just enough water to cover the meat. Simmer until they are barely tender, about 1½ hours. Remove the ribs from the pan and let them cool a bit.

Mix together the ingredients for the marinade. Brush the ribs with a little of the marinade and then put them in a deep dish and pour the remaining marinade over them. Cover the dish loosely and let the ribs sit for 1 hour. If you leave them much longer, the spices will break down.

Lay the ribs in a roasting pan fitted with a rack. Set the pan in a preheated 425°F oven and immediately lower the heat to 350°F. Cook for 20 minutes to make them crisp. Remove from the oven, cut into pieces, and serve.

Boneless Pork Roast Cooked on Top of the Stove

I often cook a pork roast or chicken on top of the stove because I find this way of cooking produces good flavor and tenderness that is different from oven cooking. Cooked in the oven, this same cut of meat would be crispy on the outside and have a very definite oven-roasted flavor. It would taste delicious, but I prefer its flavor when cooked on the stove. You also don't heat up the kitchen as much. I add peanut butter, which blends so nicely with the garlic as well as the pork, and it tastes so much better than water alone. Its flavor is a pleasant surprise.

SERVES 4 OR 5

3 pounds boneless pork roast, trimmed and tied	2 tablespoons butter
Salt and freshly ground black pepper	3 unpeeled garlic cloves
1 teaspoon ground ginger	2 tablespoons water
1 teaspoon crumbled dried sage leaves	1 to 2 tablespoons unsalted peanut butter

Cover the prepared meat with a mixture of salt, freshly ground black pepper, ginger, and sage leaves. Heat a 2-quart oval pot over medium-high heat and then warm the butter in the pot until it foams. Add the pork roast and cook it, turning constantly so that the meat is well browned all over.

Lift up the meat and place the garlic cloves on the bottom of the pot. Put the meat back on top and lower the heat so that the pork will cook without burning. Partially cover the pot so steam can escape and the meat will not stew. Adjust the heat as necessary. Cook the pork for 1½ to 2 hours, or until the meat is tender when pierced.

Remove the meat from the pot and set aside in a warm place. Skim the fat from the pot, and remove and discard the garlic. Add the water and stir to dislodge the residue that developed during cooking. Cook over low heat, adding a few more drops of water as necessary. Add 1 to 2 tablespoons of unsalted peanut butter to thicken the sauce and to add flavor. Season with more salt and pepper, if necessary. Strain the sauce and serve with the pork.

CROWN ROAST OF PORK WITH HERB DRESSING, GARNISHED WITH PINEAPPLE

If you have never served pork this way, you will find it a pretty and delicious way to do so. It looks so elegant and festive that it makes a good choice for the holidays. A crown roast is prepared for cooking by stitching together two ribbed pork loins to form a "crown" with an empty center. Ask your butcher to put the roast together for you. If the pork loins weigh 3 to 4 pounds each, you will be able to serve 4 to 6 people easily, and if some are children or light eaters, perhaps 5 to 7 or 8.

I have given a recipe for an herb dressing to fill the roast. This is an old-fashioned stuffing that tastes exactly right with the pork, especially since it includes glazed apples for sweetness, to go well with the sweet meat. It is important to prepare the bread for the dressing a day or two ahead of time by trimming the brown crusts from enough slices of good, firm white bread, when cut into ¼-inch cubes, to yield 7 cups. Good dried herbs, those that are recently bought, make the most flavorful dressing, and I also use Bell Seasoning, an old brand of poultry seasoning that has good flavor. You should be able to find it in supermarkets.

Glazed apples are made with the first summer apples as well as those available in the late fall. They may be served as a side dish with breakfast or supper, or added to a recipe such as the dressing used here. The best apples for glazing are firm varieties such as Granny Smiths, which will not fall apart during cooking. Golden Delicious work well, too.

Sweet pineapple is a great fruit to serve with pork and the golden slices look pretty on the platter with the crown roast. Pineapple slices prepared this way are also good with ham.

SERVES 4 TO 6

GLAZED APPLES

2 tablespoons butter

3 medium green apples, such as Granny Smith, Golden Delicious,

or Japanese mutsu, quartered and cored but not peeled

⅓ cup light brown sugar

(recipe continues)

¼ teaspoon salt

Scant ½ teaspoon freshly grated
   nutmeg

HERB DRESSING

7 cups white bread crumbs, a day or
   two old

1 cup finely chopped onions

1½ cups finely chopped celery

⅓ cup chopped celery leaves

2 teaspoons salt

1 teaspoon freshly ground black pepper

2 teaspoons crumbled dried sage
   leaves

1 teaspoon dried thyme leaves

1 tablespoon Bell Seasoning

1½ cups cold water

⅔ cup (1⅓ sticks) butter

CROWN ROAST

One 6- to 8-pound crown roast of pork

1 or 2 cloves garlic, peeled and cut into
   slivers

Ground ginger

Salt and freshly ground black pepper

PINEAPPLE GARNISH

1 fresh pineapple

4 teaspoons butter

1 tablespoon brown sugar

*Sheet of foil large enough to cover bottom
   of roast*

To glaze the apples: Heat the butter in a skillet until it foams. Add the apple
quarters, brown sugar, salt, and nutmeg. Cook over moderate heat, stirring
continuously, until the apples are tender and well glazed. Set aside until you
are ready to add the apples to the dressing.

To make the herb dressing: Put the bread crumbs, onions, celery, and celery
leaves in a large bowl and toss. Add the salt, pepper, sage, thyme, and Bell
Seasoning, and mix with your hands. Heat the water in a small saucepan and
when it is hot, add the butter and let it dissolve. Pour this over the crumb
mixture and mix well with your hands or a wooden spoon. Gently stir in the
apples. Cover the dressing until you are ready to fill the crown roast.

To prepare the pork roast: Make slits in the meat with the point of a sharp
knife and insert the garlic slivers. Dust the inside of the roast with ginger, salt,
and pepper. Spoon the dressing into the center of the roast. Place the sheet of
foil in a roasting pan, set the roast on it, and shape it around the bottom of
the roast. Put in a preheated 350°F oven. Be sure to adjust the oven racks so
that the roast has ample headroom. Cook for 2½ to 3 hours, until the meat

PORK LIVER PÂTÉ

After it is boiled, pork liver is rock hard and needs chicken livers ground with it for resiliency. Not every butcher today sells pork liver and you may have to order it, but the pâté is so delicious, it is worth trying to get the liver. Serve it with crackers or on toast. We made pork liver pâté every year after hog-butchering time and kept the pâté in the meat house all winter to have on hand for small snacks and for visitors. Not everybody made the pâté and ours was always popular with the neighbors.

SERVES 8

8 ounces pork liver

1 pound hog jowl or fresh bacon, in one piece

1 small onion

2 tablespoons butter

8 ounces streak-of-lean, cut into small cubes (see page 124)

1 medium to large onion (about 8 ounces), sliced

½ teaspoon dried thyme leaves

1 bay leaf

8 ounces chicken livers, cleaned

1 teaspoon finely chopped garlic

1½ teaspoons salt

1 teaspoon freshly ground black pepper

2 tablespoons brandy

Pinch crumbled dried sage leaves

15 thin strips fresh unsalted bacon

Put the pork liver, hog jowl or bacon, and small onion in a saucepan with water to cover by an inch, and simmer, covered, for 2 hours. Drain, discarding the hog jowl and reserving the liver.

Heat the butter in a skillet and when foaming, add the cubed streak-of-lean and render until the pieces are brown and crisp. Remove the pan from the burner. Spoon out the cracklings, put in the food processor, grind them to a paste, then put them in a big bowl. Put the sliced onion, thyme, and bay leaf in the pan, and sauté until the onion becomes soft, about 10 minutes. Add the chicken livers to the pan and cook, stirring, until they are just heated through, about 5 minutes. Discard the bay leaf and put the contents of the pan in a food processor; add the drained pork liver, and process to a mass. Remove to the bowl with the paste of pork cracklings, add the garlic, salt, pepper, brandy, and sage, and mix well. Taste for seasoning by sautéing a spoonful

(recipe continues)

of the pâté mixture in a small skillet with a little butter until cooked through, then taste and see if there is enough seasoning; if not, adjust as needed.

Line an 8-inch loaf pan with the strips of unsalted bacon, laying them crosswise so that when the pan is filled with the pâté you can bring together the strips on top. Pour the pâté mixture into the pan, cover with the bacon strips, then with a sheet of parchment paper that fits snugly over the top, and finally with a piece of aluminum foil, tucked in very tight. Set the pan on a rack in a larger pan and pour in enough hot water to come halfway up the sides of the loaf pan. Place in a 350°F oven and cook for 2½ hours. Remove from the oven and let cool. When cold, the pâté is ready to be unmolded and served.

Boiled Virginia Ham

A beautifully cured ham is chestnut brown and covered with a coating of black pepper as well as a moldy-looking outer covering. This outer covering, which gives the ham good flavor, is easily removed by a quick scrub under a running faucet. It has been my experience that Virginia ham tastes its very best only if it has been properly soaked before it is cooked. Some people change the water during cooking. I do not, but do change it while the ham is soaking. Preparing a Virginia ham takes time, but none of the steps is difficult. The ham would serve at least thirty at a buffet but you can prepare the ham for just a few people and then use it in a variety of ways for weeks or months to come. Use the ham bone when all the meat is gone in bean soup, such as Thirteen-Bean Soup (see page 51).

One 13- to 15-pound uncooked   *24-quart pot*
    Virginia ham
2 to 3 cups fine white bread crumbs
    (optional)

Take the ham from the protective shipping bag. (Keep the bag—it is useful as a jelly bag; see page 191.) Scrub the ham with a stiff brush under cold running water. When the moldy outer covering has been scrubbed off, rinse the ham well and then put it in the pot. Cover it with cold water and leave it in a cool spot to soak for 3 days. You do not have to refrigerate it. Change the water every day.

On the morning of the third day, drain off the soaking water and cover the ham again with clear, clean cold water. Put a lid on the pot and bring the water to a boil. Watch the pot closely and the minute the water nears the boil, turn down the heat low enough so that the water just shows a bubble. Cook the ham for approximately 5 hours, watching it to make sure the water does not get any hotter or cooler than this bubbling point. After 4½ hours, lift the ham up out of the water to see if the skin is bubbled and soft. If not, let the ham cook until the skin is soft and bubbled and ready to remove from the cooking water.

Cool the ham in a shallow pan. When it is cool enough to handle, cut the skin off with a sharp knife. As you remove the skin, trim a bit of the fat, too,

(recipe continues)

but leave a coating of fat to help keep in moisture. An edge of fat also looks nice on pieces of sliced ham and it tastes so good.

If you want to garnish the ham, sprinkle the bread crumbs over it, and heat it in a 350°F oven just long enough to brown the crumbs, about 15 minutes.

VIRGINIA HAM

Virginia hams are a little different from other cured hams because they are dry-salt-cured and then smoked. In other Southern states, where it does not get as cold, hams are cured in salt brine and then left to dry, not smoked. I have found that lots of people love to eat Virginia ham because they remember eating it years ago, but there are also those who think it tastes too strong. Virginia ham will always taste salty, but not too salty if it is cooked correctly, as I describe below. I think it's important to understand just what the ham goes through—how it is cured and hung and aged—before it's ready to cook.

There are two kinds of Virginia hams: younger ones (aged for only seven or eight months) are called Williamsburg hams; those that are aged for a year or more are called Smithfield, or sometimes country, hams. I like long-cured Smithfield the best. Both types are salted after the hogs are slaughtered and then left for about six weeks. After this time, the excess salt is shaken off and the hams are hung in a smokehouse and smoked at intervals for months, until they are cured. The older hams (Smithfield) absorb more salt and more smoky flavor. Of course, the flavor of Virginia ham, or any ham, depends on what the pig was fed in the first place.

No one who knows Virginia ham is surprised when it is served to them cold. The hams just fall apart if they are sliced warm, although I sometimes heat up a few slices in the oven. Also, no one who knows the hams is surprised by their appearance before they are cooked—all moldy and looking as though they have been buried. You have to scrub this mold off under cold running water before you soak the hams. I once left instructions for a cook who worked for me in a restaurant kitchen to soak the hams overnight. When I arrived at work the next morning, I found a note saying that the hams were bad and so he had thrown them out! He was just not used to the mold.

When you buy a Virginia ham, be sure you get one that is *not* cooked. If you do get one already cooked, slice it very thin—but even so there is a good chance the texture will be like wood. After you cook the ham, you have to skin it and cut off some of the fat. You should leave a layer of fat so that when you slice it there is a nice-looking rim of fat around the edge, just as with prosciutto. As far as slicing the hams, I think the Gwaltney Company's instructions (the company is based in Smithfield, and they send instructions with every ham) are as good as any—just remember to slice it thin. Most companies that sell Virginia hams include instructions for cooking and slicing.

After the ham is cooked, cooled, and as much as you need has been sliced off, wrap it well in parchment and foil (not plastic) and keep it in a cool room or, if you have space, the refrigerator. When I was young, we used to keep the hams in a pie safe in the pantry. That way, we always had meat, already cooked, on hand for visitors or quick meals. I usually serve the ham with Mustard with Brown Sugar (see page 122), which is sort of sweet and contrasts with the salty, dry ham. I try to serve a juicy or creamy vegetable, too, such as corn pudding, sweet potatoes, or Sautéed Bananas (see page 57). Virginia ham is delicious served in a biscuit, warm or cold. It will keep for months refrigerated; if it develops a little mold on the surface, just scrape it off.

MUSTARD WITH BROWN SUGAR

I nearly always serve this mustard with Virginia ham, although it is not a traditional accompaniment to the ham. Few people in the South ever serve mustard, but up North people ask for it. It is a spicy blend that keeps well for a month or so.

5 tablespoons dry mustard

¼ cup cider vinegar

5 tablespoons corn oil

½ teaspoon salt

½ teaspoon ground allspice

½ teaspoon ground cloves

¾ cup firmly packed brown sugar

Combine all the ingredients in the bowl of an electric mixer and mix well for 4 to 5 minutes. Set the bowl into a pan of boiling water and cook over medium heat, stirring for 15 to 20 minutes, until all the graininess disappears. Spoon the mustard into a glass jar and let it cool. Screw the lid on the jar and store the mustard in the refrigerator for at least a week before using.

SLICE OF COUNTRY HAM BAKED
WITH PINEAPPLE

I like Virginia country hams, in particular Smithfield hams, as I describe on pages 120–121. They keep in a cool place outside the refrigerator and can be brought out and sliced for a quick meal or snack. It is a good idea to paint the sliced portion of a country ham with a little melted paraffin to keep out bugs; store the ham in a cloth bag. Slices of ham are usually served cold or sliced and reheated in various ways. Sliced country ham may be fried with redeye gravy or baked in thick steaks. Their bones are used to season pea soup, chicken stews, game, and rice dishes. I like to bake a thick slice of ham with pineapple. The sweetness of the fruit and honey contrasts so well with the sharpness of the ham.

SERVES 4

1 large slice of ham, 2 inches thick, cut from the center of the ham

1 tablespoon honey

4 tablespoons (½ stick) butter, softened

2 teaspoons dry mustard

½ teaspoon ground ginger

Four or five ½-inch-thick slices fresh pineapple

1 cup water

Put the ham in a wide skillet and add enough water to cover. Bring to a near simmer and cook for 30 minutes. Lift the ham from the water and pat dry. Put the ham in a buttered baking dish and brush the top of the slice with honey. Combine the butter with the mustard and ginger, and paint the ham with the butter mixture. Lay the pineapple slices on top of the ham and add the water. Bake in a preheated 325°F oven for 1½ hours. Arrange the ham and pineapple slices on a platter and spoon the pan juices over both. Serve hot.

Streak-of-Lean, Salt Pork, and Bacon

A lot of people recommend using salt pork but do not distinguish it from fatback, which has very little flavor. I think you should always use a piece of salt pork that has a streak of lean running through it—a lean line of meat showing. Streak-of-lean, as this kind of salt pork is called, is from the same part of the pig (the belly) as bacon but it is not cured and smoked. Streak-of-lean is simply put in brine and then allowed to dry. Bacon is put down in salt and then smoked. Fresh bacon is different from either one. It is neither salted nor smoked.

The French use streak-of-lean a lot in cooking, too, just as we always did when I was growing up, and as I still do today. I think it adds good flavor to all sorts of different dishes. Although you can get it at some supermarkets, the butcher will certainly have it. Sometimes you can substitute cured bacon for streak-of-lean, but not always. For instance, you would not use bacon for many pâtés because of the smoky flavor.

Rabbit

Rabbit has not been eaten much in this country for the past 20 years or so, but when I was younger we ate it all the time. I do not think it has a very distinctive flavor—to me it tastes rather like chicken—but it blends well with other flavors. Rabbits were plentiful when I was a child and we would trap them nearly all year long. The traps did not kill them, just captured them. Most everybody living in the countryside ate rabbit, but always wild rabbit—nobody raised it for food. Nowadays, rabbit is once again becoming common and you can buy it in most supermarkets. If you know that the rabbit you buy is very fresh, it is a good idea to hold it a few days in the refrigerator before cooking.

Rabbit Pâté

I have been cooking rabbit a lot lately and have found that this pâté is the best way to bring out the flavor. I seem to make it about every other week, everyone just likes it so much. The chicken livers keep it from being too dry, but you have to be careful that their flavor does not overwhelm the rabbit. The streak-of-lean is important, too, for good flavor, as is the garlic. Before you bone out the rabbit, let the meat stiffen a little in the freezer to make boning easier. Be sure to go over the rabbit meat very carefully to take out all the fine bones. The recipe makes a lot of pâté and, if you want, you can halve it. However, if you make it all, simply wrap what you do not use in parchment and foil and freeze it. It keeps in the freezer for a few months.

MAKES TWO 8-INCH LOAVES

4 tablespoons (½ stick) butter
10 ounces streak-of-lean, cut into ½-inch cubes
2 teaspoons dried thyme leaves
2 medium bay leaves, broken into pieces
1 pound onions, sliced
8 ounces chicken livers
2 tablespoons brandy

5 pounds boned rabbit meat
1 tablespoon finely chopped garlic
Salt
2 teaspoons freshly ground black pepper
2 teaspoons Provence herbs
1 teaspoon ground allspice
3 pounds sliced fresh unsalted bacon

Heat a 10-inch frying pan, and add the butter. When the butter foams, add the cubed streak-of-lean, thyme, and bay leaves. Cook this mixture over medium-high heat, stirring all the while. The streak-of-lean must become brown and crisp. Using a slotted spoon, remove the defatted pieces from the pan and add the onions. Stir until the onions are soft and light brown, then add the chicken livers. Stir until the livers are quite seared, yet pink inside. Add the brandy, set it on fire, and when it has burned off, remove the pan from the burner. Spoon the liver mixture into a bowl, and set aside. Coarsely grind the rabbit meat and spoon it into a large mixing bowl. Grind the liver and onion mixture, then grind the defatted streak-of-lean pieces fine, and add all the ground ingredients to the bowl with the rabbit. Sprinkle in the garlic, salt, pepper, Provence herbs, and allspice. Take two large forks and thoroughly mix the ingredients. To test for seasoning, heat a little butter in a small skillet, then add a small thin cake of the pâté mixture. Brown on both sides, and taste carefully for seasoning; correct if needed. Let the pâté mixture rest while you line two 8-inch loaf pans with the unsalted bacon slices. Fill the lined pans with the mixture, then cover the pâté with more bacon slices. Trim the edges so the slices are flush with the pan. Cut pieces of parchment paper to fit over each pan. Then cut pieces of aluminum foil to cover and pinch them down closely. In a large baking pan, put a cake rack or skewers to set the pans on so they are not resting on the bottom of the pan. Pour in enough boiling water to come halfway up sides of the pans. Cover with a sheet of foil and set in a preheated 350°F oven for 2½ hours. Remove from the oven. Uncover, lift out pans, and set them on a wire rack to cool. When cooled, place a 2-pound weight on each pan. Place in the refrigerator; the next day remove the weights, and let the pâté rest 5 days in a cold place before serving. Kept in a cold spot, the pâté will keep 2 weeks or more. The flavor develops with age.

FRIED RABBIT

I like to fry the forelegs and the ribbed side pieces of the rabbit. The forelegs have less meat than the hind legs and seem to do better fried with smoked ham and a little seasoning to bring out the flavor. If you season rabbit with too many herbs, its flavor is lost. This method of frying is not especially quick, but I have found slow cooking is best for rabbit.

SERVES 4

4 forelegs of rabbit
4 side pieces of rabbit
1 teaspoon salt
½ teaspoon freshly ground black
  pepper

1 cup flour
½ cup butter and home-rendered lard,
  mixed
1 slice Virginia ham, cut into 2 pieces
⅓ cup water

Rinse the rabbit pieces under cold water. Wipe dry and sprinkle the pieces with salt and pepper, then drop each piece, one at the time, into a paper bag containing the flour. Shake the bag up to coat each piece well with flour. Lay each piece on a piece of wax paper until ready to cook.

Heat a 9-inch cast-iron skillet and add the butter and lard mixture and the piece of ham. Heat to foaming, then add the rabbit. Keep the pan hot enough to brown the pieces but not to burn them. Turn them when well browned. Turn the ham also, and place it on top of the rabbit pieces until the cooking is finished. After the rabbit has browned on both sides, add the water, swishing the pan around to make sure the water is mixed in. Cover lightly, and turn heat very low. Simmer for 1½ hours, until tender. Discard the ham before serving.

BRAISED RABBIT

Braising is a method of cooking older, bigger rabbits that need long cooking for tenderizing. When I was young, these big rabbits were always in the garden or someplace equally visible. I use the hind legs in this recipe as well as the saddle. The hind legs are meatier and fattier than the forelegs and add more flavor to the stew.

SERVES 4

2 hind legs of rabbit

2 saddle pieces of rabbit

½ teaspoon salt

¼ teaspoon freshly ground black
  pepper

1 cup flour

½ cup (1 stick) plus 2 tablespoons
  butter

One ½-inch slice Virginia ham

2 teaspoons vinegar

1 medium onion, sliced

½ teaspoon dried thyme leaves

Sprig parsley

¼ teaspoon finely chopped garlic

4 large cultivated or wild mushrooms

Season the rabbit pieces with the salt and pepper. Put the flour in a paper bag and dust the rabbit pieces by shaking them, one at a time, in the bag. Lay the rabbit pieces on wax paper until ready to cook. Heat ½ cup butter in a heavy 2-quart pot until foaming, add the ham and rabbit, and brown on both sides. Add the vinegar, sliced onion, and thyme, and continue searing for 15 minutes. Add the parsley and turn the heat down to a simmer, cover closely, and cook for 2 hours, or until the meat is tender. Stir in the garlic 20 minutes before the rabbit is finished. Meanwhile sauté the mushrooms in the remaining 2 tablespoons butter in a small skillet, tossing them, for about 5 minutes. Use the mushrooms as a garnish on each serving and serve with quick-cooked green beans and crusty bread.

STUFFED RABBIT

Stuffing a rabbit turns it into a meal with nice, strong flavor. Rabbit and pork are a good combination—use any lean pork in the market, such as boneless loin chops or tenderloin. For the pork fat, cut up fresh (uncured) bacon, available through most butchers and supermarkets. Muscat raisins appear in the markets in the fall and are sold in clusters all wrapped in cellophane or sold loose.

SERVES 4

STUFFING

2 tablespoons butter

1 cup cubed streak-of-lean (see page 124)

1½ cups chopped onions

4 chicken livers

2 tablespoons cognac

½ pound fresh lean pork, roughly chopped

½ pound fresh pork fat, from fresh bacon, roughly chopped

1½ teaspoons dried thyme leaves

2 teaspoons salt, or to taste

1 teaspoon freshly ground black pepper

½ cup halved hazelnuts

½ cup Muscat raisins, seeded

RABBIT

One 5-pound rabbit

1 cup (2 sticks) butter

Salt and freshly ground black pepper

Dried thyme leaves

1 medium onion, sliced

½ teaspoon chopped garlic

1 cup water or white wine

Heat a large skillet over high heat and melt the butter. When it begins to foam, add the cubed streak-of-lean, and cook until crispy. Lift the streak-of-lean from the pan with a slotted spoon and set aside.

Pour off half the fat, add the onions to the skillet and sauté for 3 or 4 minutes, then add the chicken livers. Cook them just to sear and remove the pan from the heat. Pour the cognac over the livers and ignite it. When the flames die out, put the liver and onions in a food processor and process quickly, just to blend. Remove the liver and onions from the processor and add the streak-of-lean cubes. Process the streak-of-lean to a paste and set it aside.

Put the lean and fat pork in the processor and grind coarsely. Put the ground pork in a bowl and add the liver and onions, the streak-of-lean paste, the seasonings, hazelnuts, and raisins. Test the flavor of the stuffing before spooning it into the rabbit by frying a small, thin cake and tasting it. Adjust the seasonings if necessary.

Preheat the oven to 375°F.

Spoon the stuffing into the rabbit and pin it together with small skewers. Lace the skewers with twine so they are securely in place. Heat the butter in an oblong pot until it foams. Put the rabbit in the pot and sear on all sides until browned, which should take 10 to 12 minutes. Sprinkle the rabbit lightly with salt, pepper, and thyme. Scatter the onion slices over the rabbit. Add the garlic and water to the pot, cover, and cook for 1½ hours. Test for doneness by piercing the rabbit with a fork—it should feel tender. Remove the rabbit from the pot, place it on a warmed platter, and spoon the ingredients from the pot over the rabbit. Serve at once.

BEEF TENDERLOIN WITH BÉARNAISE SAUCE

When beef tenderloin is seasoned with freshly cracked black pepper and crushed garlic, grilled or broiled so that it is crusty outside and rare and juicy inside, and then served with béarnaise sauce, it is one of the most delicious dishes I know.

Béarnaise sauce has truly rare flavor. Similar to hollandaise, which I also love, it gets its fabulous taste from a combination of fresh herbs. I have to admit that I cook beef tenderloin just so I can have béarnaise. The herbs have to be fresh; dried chervil and tarragon taste like dried-out grass. Neither herb is hard to find fresh these days—sometimes you can find them in supermarkets.

I make béarnaise with the pan sitting directly on the burner, but if you are a little afraid of this, use a double boiler. Heat the water in the double boiler to a simmer and keep it there while you are cooking the sauce. It is important that the butter is cold when it is added because the reaction of the cold butter to the hot liquid helps the sauce thicken and develop its consistency. When you are salting the sauce, keep in mind that the meat is not salted—but also take care not to oversalt. As soon as the sauce thickens, set the pan in a bowl of ice-cold water to stop the cooking. This way, the sauce should not separate.

SERVES 4, WITH ABOUT ¼ CUP SAUCE PER SERVING

BEEF TENDERLOIN

    2 teaspoons freshly cracked black pepper

    1 teaspoon crushed garlic

    Four 6-ounce beef tenderloins

BÉARNAISE SAUCE

    ¼ cup white wine

    6 tablespoons white wine vinegar

    1 rounded tablespoon finely chopped shallots

    2 tablespoons finely chopped fresh tarragon

    1 tablespoon finely chopped chervil leaves and
        stems

    ⅔ cup (1⅓ sticks) cold butter

    3 egg yolks

1 teaspoon salt

¼ teaspoon cayenne

1 tablespoon finely cut fresh tarragon

1 tablespoon finely cut chervil

Mix together the pepper and crushed garlic and rub the mixture over the tenderloins. Cook the beef over a hot grill or under a broiler for 5 to 6 minutes on each side to get it crusty on the outside but still rare inside.

Meanwhile make the béarnaise sauce: Put the wine, vinegar, shallots, tarragon, and chervil in a 1-quart nonmetallic heavy saucepan. Set it over medium-low heat, and simmer until the liquid has nearly evaporated—that is, leaving about 1 tablespoon of liquid. Remove from the burner. Cut the butter into 4 equal pieces and put it near the stove. Put the 3 egg yolks near the stove also. Have ready a large bowl of ice water. Now, with a wire whisk in hand, set the pan with the wine and herb reduction over medium heat. Add 1 piece of the butter and 1 egg yolk, whisking all the while. When the butter has been incorporated, add another egg yolk and another piece of butter, whisking continuously until the butter has been incorporated, then repeat. Finally whisk in the remaining butter, and in about 3 minutes, stirring constantly and lifting the pan from the heat now and then, the sauce will have thickened to the consistency of a hollandaise. When the sauce is thick, remove the pan from the heat and set it in a bowl of ice water to stop the cooking. Stir well and pour the sauce through a sieve into a bowl, season with salt and cayenne, and stir in the finely cut fresh herbs. Do not refrigerate. Pass with the fillet.

Three

FROM
THE LAKES,
STREAMS,
AND
OCEANS

Red Snapper with Olive Mayonnaise

Stuffed Red Snapper

  Buying Fish

Flounder in Parchment with Mixed Vegetables

Sautéed Fillet of Flounder in Butter and Garlic

Shallot Butter

Shrimp Sautéed with Butter, Garlic, and Parsley

Shrimp Paste

Soft-shell Crabs

Herring Fillet in Cream Sauce with Garlic, Tarragon, and White Wine

Herring Roe

Panfried Virginia Spots

Catfish Stew

Eels and Scallops

Tartar Sauce

Herb Sauce for Fish

Oyster Stew with Salsify, Garnished with Finely Cut Parsley

Panfried Oysters with Cornmeal Coating

Escalloped Oysters

She-Crab Soup with Rice and a Garnish of Finely Cut Parsley

She-Crab Soup, Charleston Style

  Crabmeat

Fresh Crabmeat with Light Mayonnaise

Deviled Crab

Hearty Fish Chowder

Panfried Trout

Broiled Mackerel

Buying Fish

It may not be very polite, but you should smell fish to know whether to buy it. If fish is fresh it will smell like the sea and have no stale odor at all. Nothing tastes worse than a stale fish. When you are lucky enough to taste just-caught fish, not even a day old, you realize how good it is. There is nothing like it. If possible, buy fish whole and then, if necessary, ask the fishmonger to fillet it for you. The eyes on a fresh fish are bulging, not sunken. Look at the fish's gills—they should be deep red, not pale or pink. If you have not had the opportunity to smell the fish and its odor is very strong when you unwrap it at home, take it back—it isn't fresh. It is always a good idea to take fish from the wrapper as soon as you get home and rewrap it in parchment or wax paper and store it in the refrigerator until you are ready to cook it. This way you can be sure it is well insulated. Cook the fish as soon as you can, on the same day you buy it.

FLOUNDER IN PARCHMENT WITH MIXED VEGETABLES

I really like to cook in parchment. It looks so pretty and is an exciting way to present food. Many people like foil, too, but I do not like the idea of acidic wine against the foil. Parchment holds in aromas and moisture and just makes everything taste very good. It is a particularly good way to cook fish because it is so gentle and moist. I like to use flounder in this recipe, a fish that's common in Southern waters and one that I have eaten for a long time. If you cannot get it, substitute sole, which is a little lighter but equally good. Adding mixed vegetables makes the fish colorful and pretty; you can use any combination of the vegetables suggested as long as you keep an even mixture of white, yellow, and green. Cook the flounder in individual parchment paper packets or in one large piece that is about 23 by 16 inches. When you bring the packets to the table, snip them open right in front of the guests so that the aroma bursts out. It creates a wonderful, festive feeling.

SERVES 5

½ pound green beans

2 medium carrots

2 medium parsnips

5 flounder fillets, about 4 ounces each

Juice of 1 lemon

½ cup (1 stick) butter, softened

15 slices medium onions (3 for each packet)

2 teaspoons salt mixed with 1 teaspoon dried thyme leaves and 1 teaspoon freshly ground black pepper

2 tablespoons finely chopped parsley

5 thin slices chilled butter

½ cup plus 2 tablespoons white wine

Wash and drain the beans, carrots, and parsnips. If the parsnips have woody centers, cut them out and use an extra half parsnip to make up the loss. Snip the ends off the beans and scrape the carrots and parsnips with a vegetable peeler. Cut all the vegetables to the same length—about 2½ inches—then cut each piece into very thin sticks, no thicker than a kitchen matchstick. The fish requires very little cooking, so the vegetables must be cut very thin.

Wipe each piece of flounder with a clean, damp cloth. Place on a flat dish and squeeze a few drops of lemon juice over each fillet.

Take one 18-by-15-inch sheet of parchment paper. Spread about 1½ table-spoons of the softened butter over the center of the sheet, covering a 4-inch square. Place 3 slices of onion on top of the butter. Arrange a fish fillet over the onion slices, curving it slightly. Sprinkle about ½ teaspoon of the salt mixture over each fish. Mound one-fifth of the chopped, mixed vegetables on top and add a good pinch of chopped parsley. Dot with 1 slice of the cold butter and sprinkle again with parsley. Take one corner of the parchment and gather the paper together, working in a clockwise direction and holding it tight as you form it into a pouch. Before closing completely, splash 2 tablespoons of white wine into the pouch. Close each pouch and tie securely with a piece of string. Prepare the remaining 4 packages in the same way.

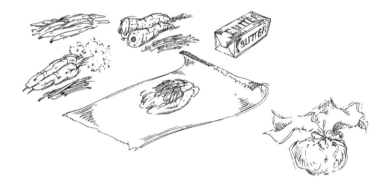

Set the pouches on a large cookie sheet so that they do not touch each other, and refrigerate them—they can be prepared a few hours ahead of time.

Preheat the oven to 400°F.

Put the tray of fish packets in the oven, turn the heat up to 425°F, and bake for 17 minutes. Rush each packet to the table on a plate and cut the pouches with a sharp pair of scissors so that the aroma is released right before your guests.

Sautéed Fillet of Flounder in Butter and Garlic

This recipe could not be more simple or more delicious. Its simplicity lies in beginning with very fresh fish, coating the fillets with flour and letting them rest so the flour adheres, and having the skillet hot and the butter foaming when you lay the fillets in the pan. Sauté them quickly over medium-high heat and then serve them directly from the stove. Except for foods such as stews, most things should be served right away—when they are just finished cooking and still very hot. Otherwise their flavor and texture change. As a restaurant cook, the first thing I do when I begin working in a new kitchen is to remove all the heat lamps and any other devices that keep cooked food warm. I like to serve right from the stove in a restaurant as well as at home. Everything just tastes better.

SERVES 4

4 flounder fillets (approximately 8 ounces each)	1 teaspoon salt
	Freshly ground black pepper
Juice of ½ lemon	4 tablespoons (½ stick) butter
1 cup flour	¼ teaspoon very finely chopped garlic

Wipe the fillets off with a clean, damp cloth. Lay them on a dish and squeeze the lemon juice over the pieces. Let them rest while preparing the rest of the dish. Put the flour on a sheet of wax paper and mix in the salt and pepper. Mix well and lightly press the fillets into the flour, coating both sides. Lay the floured pieces on the sheet of wax paper and let rest for 30 minutes to 1 hour. If the fillets are a bit sticky after resting, press them again lightly into the flour and shake off the excess.

Heat a skillet that is large enough to hold all of the fillets, and add the butter. When the butter foams and begins to brown, add the garlic. See that it is scattered over the pan. Then quickly add the fillets, cut side down. Cook over medium-high heat until the flounder is a golden brown color, and turn over. Then set the pan in a preheated 350°F oven while finishing the rest of the meal. Total cooking time should be about 10 minutes. Remove the pan from the oven and put the fish on a hot plate. Serve immediately.

Herring Fillet in Cream Sauce with Garlic, Tarragon, and White Wine

I think many people don't like fresh herring because they are afraid of all the bones. But if you fillet the fish carefully, the bones are not a problem. As the herring's early spring season is so brief, it is a good idea to order ahead from a fish store. We never had fish stores when I was young, so we were eager to catch fresh herring every spring. Southern herring is a broad fish with bright, shiny scales and sweet, light flesh. I poach the fillets in a little wine for no longer than 2 minutes and garnish with a Bombay mango. Bombay mangoes are the flat ones and their sweet flavor and silky texture set off the taste of the fish.

SERVES 5 OR 6

6 herring, filleted (12 pieces)

½ cup white wine

1 cup water

5 tarragon leaves

3 large mushrooms, sliced

¼ teaspoon finely scraped garlic

2 tablespoons butter

½ cup heavy cream

Sprig tarragon

1 Bombay mango, sliced

6 stalks of scallion, for garnish

In a large skillet that will hold the fillets in one layer, poach the fillets in the wine, water, and tarragon for 2 minutes. Meanwhile, sauté the mushrooms and garlic in butter for 2 to 3 minutes. Remove the fillets to a hot dish and boil the liquid down to ½ cup. Pour the cream into the liquid and boil again for a few minutes to thicken, then pour over the fillets. Garnish with a sprig of tarragon, slices of mango, the scallions, and the mushrooms.

Herring Roe

I am most familiar with the herring sold in the South, where the roe is considered a delicacy. I like herring roe even better than shad roe. Both are available only in the early spring and I always buy herring roe the minute I see it in the stores. If I am not planning to eat it right away, I wrap it well and freeze it. This is the only fish I freeze. I sauté the roe in butter and flavor it with lemon and parsley and a just a little garlic and eat it for lunch or as an appetizer.

SERVES 4 AS AN APPETIZER

⅓ cup (⅔ stick) butter

½ teaspoon finely chopped garlic

12 roe, approximately 2½ to 3 inches long and ½ inch thick

2 tablespoons finely cut parsley

Juice of ½ lemon

Salt and freshly ground black pepper

Heat a wide, heavy skillet, then add the butter. When the butter foams and begins to brown on the edges, sprinkle in the garlic. Add the roe, sear on each side, and sauté for 3 to 4 minutes, just until done. Add parsley and squeeze lemon juice over the roe. Add salt and pepper to taste. The dish should be well seasoned with the flavor of parsley, lemon, salt, and pepper, and there should be just enough garlic to give a good flavor.

PANFRIED VIRGINIA SPOTS

Virginia spots are the sweetest scaled fish I know. They are pale gray and lightly textured, and while they have bones, they aren't as bony as many. It's the bone that gives them such good flavor. I have found them in the markets from early spring until September and have always felt the best way to cook them is fried. I score each fish three times on both sides, roll them in cornmeal, and then fry them in hot lard or butter until they are crisp all over. All you need to serve with them is a wedge of lemon. They are sold in other parts of the country and I have not found a fish that can be substituted for them.

SERVES 4

4 whole Virginia spots, cleaned	½ cup butter or lard
Salt and freshly ground black pepper	4 lemon wedges
1 cup cornmeal	

Sprinkle the fish, inside and out, with salt and pepper. Put the cornmeal on a plate, mix in 1 teaspoon salt and ½ teaspoon pepper, and roll the fish in it to coat both sides.

Heat the butter or lard in a frying pan large enough to hold all 4 fish at once. When the fat is very hot, add the fish and cook briskly over high heat for about 10 minutes on both sides. Drain on paper towels and serve hot with the lemon wedges.

CATFISH STEW

Whenever Mother got hold of some catfish, she would quickly skin them and fry them up for supper. We all loved catfish cooked this way, but after I grew up and left home, I never felt it tasted quite the same. I have looked for ways of preparing it that are a little more interesting than fried and I think this simple stew is about the best. (Fried catfish is always good but I have never tasted any as good as my mother's.) In the stew, the flavor of the fish is strong enough to stand up to the vegetables and seasonings, although the stew does not taste overwhelmingly of fish. If you have never tasted catfish, I think this would be a good recipe to start with.

SERVES 4

4 tablespoons (½ stick) butter

3 slices bacon, cut into cubes

3 pounds fresh catfish, skinned, cleaned, boned, and cut into 6 to 8 pieces

½ teaspoon dried thyme leaves

1 medium onion, sliced

3 scallions, white and 2 inches of green, sliced

1 clove garlic, smashed

1 cup peeled, seeded, and roughly chopped ripe tomatoes

½ cup sliced carrots

2 or 3 sprigs parsley

1 cup cold water

1 teaspoon freshly ground black pepper

1 teaspoon salt

1 tablespoon chopped parsley

Heat 1 tablespoon of butter in a heavy enamel or stainless steel skillet until foaming. Add the bacon, and cook until crisp. Remove the bacon from the skillet, drain, and set aside.

Wash the pieces of fish under running water and pat them dry. Heat the rest of the butter until it foams, add the thyme, and then sear the catfish pieces well. When well seared, remove the catfish to a platter.

Add the onion, scallions, and garlic to the pan, and sauté for 2 to 3 minutes, until the onion softens a little. Add the tomatoes, carrots, sprigs of parsley, and water, and stir well. Add the catfish and bacon pieces. Season with the pepper, cover, and cook the stew slowly over low heat on top of the stove for 25 minutes. Remove the sprigs of parsley and taste for seasoning. Add the salt and sprinkle with chopped parsley.

Herb Sauce for Fish

MAKES ABOUT 1 CUP

2 tablespoons vinegar

1 tablespoon white wine

1 tablespoon chopped shallots

1 tablespoon chopped fresh tarragon

2 egg yolks

5 tablespoons butter, cut into pieces

⅓ cup tomato purée

1 tablespoon finely chopped parsley

Salt and freshly ground black pepper

Put the vinegar, white wine, shallots, and tarragon in a saucepan, and simmer over low heat until the liquid is nearly evaporated. Add the egg yolks and the pieces of butter, stirring until thickened. Stir in the tomato purée and parsley, and season to taste with salt and pepper. Serve warm.

OYSTER STEW WITH SALSIFY, GARNISHED WITH FINELY CUT PARSLEY

Buying oysters is chancy and it's always best to buy them in their shells. Sometimes the liquid from canned oysters looks pink or dull gray and you don't know how long the oysters have been in the can. Ask for enough oysters to make 1½ quarts and then stand right there while they are shucked. Or, ask the fishmonger to open them and leave them in the shells, which is what I do if I don't have time to shuck them myself. The oysters for this recipe are seared and browned a little to heighten their flavor and add to the overall taste of the stew. Don't worry about exactly how much liquor you get from the oysters. Use what you have; it is for flavor.

Salsify has the taste of oysters and so I add it to the stew to give it some extra flavor. It also adds texture, similar to that of a carrot. Drop the salsify in the milk the minute you peel it so it won't turn brown.

I specify good sherry in the recipe because if you use cheap sherry you have to add so much you kill the taste of whatever you are cooking. I feel the same way about wine and often open one of the bottles that will be drunk with the meal to use in the cooking. With cheap wine, cheap sherry, cheap anything, you cannot get good flavor.

SERVES 8

1 cup peeled and chopped salsify	1 cup half-and-half
Milk and water	Aged sherry to taste
1½ quarts fresh shucked oysters and	Salt and cayenne
their liquor	5 tablespoons butter
3 cups milk	2 teaspoons finely cut parsley
1 cup heavy cream	

You may chop the salsify any way you want to, but I would cut it into ½-inch-long sticks sliced on the bias. As soon as the salsify is cut, drop it in a pan with an even mixture of milk and water to cover. Simmer rapidly for 15 minutes.

Drain the oysters, reserving the liquor. Heat the liquor in a saucepan. When hot, add the milk, cream, and half-and-half. Stir well. Add the sherry and continue to heat without boiling. Drain the salsify and add it to the pan. Season with salt and cayenne.

At the last minute before serving, melt the butter in a wide skillet. When the skillet is hot and the butter begins to brown without burning, toss in the well-drained oysters. Keep the flame high to sear the oysters, stirring all the while, and cook for about 3 minutes. Spoon the oysters into the hot milk and salsify mixture. Heat without boiling. Serve in warmed soup bowls. Garnish each bowl with ¼ teaspoon finely cut parsley, and serve with Benne Seed Biscuits (see page 209).

NOTE:
A good, simple way to open oysters is to take a beer can opener, press it into the hinge, and pry the shell open.

Panfried Oysters with Cornmeal Coating

My mother would always make fried oysters for Christmas breakfast when I was young. Right before Christmas was about the only time we could get oysters and we ate them as often as possible during the holidays.

SERVES 5 OR 6

4 eggs, beaten
1 teaspoon salt
½ teaspoon freshly ground black pepper
2 tablespoons peanut oil
2 cups white cornmeal seasoned with ½ teaspoon
    each salt and freshly ground black pepper
1 quart shucked oysters, drained
2 tablespoons bacon fat, from 4 or 5 slices bacon
⅓ cup lard

Put the beaten eggs in a bowl and add the salt, pepper, and oil. Spread the seasoned cornmeal on a sheet of wax paper. Using a fork, dip each oyster first in the egg and then the cornmeal. Be sure the cornmeal coating is light. Set the coated oysters on a platter and let them stand for 5 or 6 minutes before cooking.

Heat the bacon fat and lard in a wide skillet over high heat until nearly smoking. Add the oysters, and fry for 3 to 4 seconds a side, until golden. Drain well on a clean towel and keep hot in the oven until ready to serve. Garnish with bacon, if you like.

Escalloped Oysters

We always had oysters during the Christmas holidays when I was growing up, eating them fried for breakfast and escalloped for Christmas dinner. We would buy the oysters already shucked from the store, where they were kept in big barrels ready to be scooped into our waiting buckets and carried home. I can never think of Christmas today without remembering how good those oysters tasted. I think it is best nowadays to buy oysters in the shells for this and any other oyster recipe to be sure you get the freshest ones possible. Be sure to drain the oysters well on clean, dry towels—dry oysters are the secret to the success of this dish.

SERVES 4

1½ quarts fresh shucked oysters

10 slices white bread

Salt and freshly ground black pepper

½ cup (1 stick) butter

3 tablespoons heavy cream

3 tablespoons good sherry

Drain the oysters on a clean towel until very dry. Toast the bread slices until light brown, trim the crusts, and crush the toast in a blender or food processor to make crumbs. You should have about 3 cups of crumbs. Butter an 8-by-8-by-2-inch glass baking dish well and press a third of the bread crumbs into the bottom. Next, spread half the oysters over the crumbs and sprinkle lightly with salt and pepper. Add another layer of crumbs and then the rest of the oysters and season them with salt and pepper. Top with the remaining bread crumbs and dot all over with small pieces of butter. Sprinkle the cream and sherry over the casserole and place in a preheated 350°F oven. Bake, uncovered, for 25 to 30 minutes. Take from the oven and serve hot.

SHE-CRAB SOUP WITH RICE AND A GARNISH OF FINELY CUT PARSLEY

Crabs are the sweetest shellfish in the sea. I have never tasted a crab dish I didn't love. Only female crabs have a pointed apron flap on their bellies and their roe adds rich flavor and explains the name of this soup. If you must, use male crabs as well as female, but in any event, be sure the crabs are very much alive when you buy them. Dead crabs may make you sick—I throw out even the weak ones. This version of she-crab soup is a little different from the Charleston-style soup that follows and is every bit as good. It will serve 6 people easily as a main course and 8 as a first course or light meal.

SERVES 6 TO 8

24 lively hard-shell blue crabs, female
  if possible
½ cup bacon fat
2½ cups chopped onions
3 cloves garlic, crushed
2 teaspoons dried thyme leaves
2 bay leaves
12 ripe tomatoes, peeled, seeded, and
  chopped (about 4 cups)

1 tablespoon finely chopped hot red or
  green seeded pepper
12 cups (3 quarts) water
Salt and freshly ground black pepper
2 tablespoons finely chopped parsley
2 cups warm cooked Carolina or
  popcorn rice
Sprigs fresh thyme, for garnish
  (optional)

Spill the live crabs into the kitchen sink and, using a pair of tongs, rinse each one under running water. Do not plug the sink. Pour a kettle of boiling water over the crabs in the sink to quiet and sterilize them. When they cool down

NOTE:

The mayonnaise may be doubled to yield about 2 cups. You may flavor it by adding 1 to 2 tablespoons of finely chopped chervil, tarragon, basil, chives, or watercress, or any combination of these herbs. Stir them into the mayonnaise well. If you double the recipe, increase the amount of herbs to 3 tablespoons.

To make the mayonnaise in a blender, put all the ingredients except the oil in the blender jar. Add the oil in a steady stream through the opening in the top of the jar while the machine is running.

DEVILED CRAB

Crabmeat is delicious no matter how it is prepared. The way we prepared deviled crab when I was growing up is very simple, and the wonderful flavor remains in my memory. Serve it as an appetizer stuffed into scallop shells.

SERVES 8

4 slices firm white bread, crusts removed	2 whole eggs
⅓ cup melted butter	Salt and freshly ground black pepper
2 pounds crabmeat, picked free of shell and cartilage	Cayenne
	½ cup chopped onion

Place the bread in a flat dish and pour the melted butter evenly over it. Let soak for 25 minutes. Pull the bread apart with two forks.

Put the crabmeat in a bowl. Add the bread and the eggs. Mix well with your fingers. Season to taste with salt, pepper, and cayenne. Add the onion and mix thoroughly. Stuff the mixture into scallop shells or small decorative ramekins. Bake in a preheated 350°F oven for 25 minutes and serve right away.

HEARTY FISH CHOWDER

I developed this recipe for someone who wanted a big, hearty soup for a Christmas Eve party. Because the soup can be prepared the day before serving and only the clams and oysters are added at the last minute during heating, it is perfect for a large party and needs nothing more than salad and bread as accompaniments. I call it a chowder because of the potatoes and also because the large pieces of fish help make it thick and hearty, characteristics I associate with chowder. If you can, buy a cod collar and cod head to make the stock. The collar is a bone just below the head and makes an especially flavorful broth. You have to buy it at a fish store—you will never see one in a supermarket—but the fishmonger should know what you mean when you ask for it.

SERVES 10

4 tablespoons (½ stick) butter
½ pound streak-of-lean, cut into small cubes (see page 124)
1 cod collar and head, if available
1 medium onion, peeled
2 stalks celery with leaves
3 sprigs parsley
2 bay leaves, broken into pieces
1½ teaspoons dried thyme leaves
1 pound haddock or halibut
2 pounds codfish fillet, in one piece
⅔ cup chopped onions

⅔ cup leeks, cut in small pieces, with ½ inch of green top
2 cups diced white potatoes
2 quarts milk
2 cups heavy cream (not ultra-pasteurized)
Salt and freshly ground black pepper
6 to 8 drops Tabasco, or ¼ teaspoon cayenne
1 pint fresh shucked clams
1 pint fresh shucked oysters
½ cup Chablis or other dry white wine

Heat a large skillet, then add 1 tablespoon of the butter and the cubed streak-of-lean. Cook until the pork is rendered of fat and the cubes are crisp. Remove the defatted pieces and set aside. Add the cod collar and head, if using, and sear well on both sides without browning. Remove the contents of the pan to a large pot and add the onion, celery, and herbs. Pour in cold water to cover. Add the haddock and the codfish fillet last. Bring the liquid to a simmer and let simmer 15 minutes. Remove the fish to a bowl and cover. Continue to cook the rest 1 hour longer. Strain the stock into a bowl, cover, and discard the solids. Pour the strained stock into a pot and set over low heat. Heat a skillet and add the rest of the butter, then the chopped onions, leeks, and potatoes. Cook for a few minutes without browning. Turn the vegetables into the stock. Stir in the milk and cream, and cook gently for 30 minutes. Break up the reserved fish into small pieces and add them to the chowder. Season to taste with salt and pepper and Tabasco. You may prepare the chowder up to this point one day ahead. Reheat and add the clams 15 minutes before serving and the oysters 10 minutes later. Taste and correct the seasoning, and stir in the dry white wine. Reheat the defatted pork pieces briefly in the oven and garnish the chowder with them.

PANFRIED TROUT

A lot of the trout available today is raised on fish farms and so is easily available. The best-tasting trout, of course, is freshly caught and immediately cooked. Trout has a wonderful flavor and I think the fish always ought to be cooked whole. You will need one whole fish for each serving. It tastes really delicious with black walnuts, but since they are often hard to find, you may substitute English walnuts for a different but still good flavor.

SERVES 4

4 medium trout, cleaned
Salt and freshly ground black pepper
4 sprigs fennel, if available, or parsley
2 cups flour seasoned with 1 teaspoon
    freshly ground black pepper and
    3 teaspoons salt

½ cup (1 stick) butter
1 small clove garlic, scraped
1 cup finely chopped walnuts,
    preferably black walnuts
¼ cup finely chopped parsley

Wash the trout inside and out under cold running water and pat them dry. Sprinkle the cavity of each fish with salt and pepper and stuff with a sprig of fennel or parsley.

Put the seasoned flour in a wide shallow pan. Press each trout into the seasoned flour and set on wax paper until ready to cook.

Melt the butter in a wide skillet over medium-high heat. Add the garlic and cook briefly. Add the trout when the butter begins to foam. Be very careful when frying the fish. The flame should be rather high, but be sure not to burn the fish. Cook for 4 to 5 minutes.

Turn the trout with a spatula. They should be well browned. Sprinkle each fish with a coating of chopped walnuts and cook the second side for about 4 minutes. Remove the fish to a hot platter and sprinkle with parsley. Raise the heat so the fat in the pan gets very hot. Spoon a little of the fat over each trout and serve.

BROILED MACKEREL

Mackerel is a full-bodied fish that tastes best when just caught. However, not too many people are lucky enough to get fresh-caught mackerel, so you should be sure to buy it as fresh as possible from a reliable shop rather than frozen. It is delicious baked whole (the bones give good flavor) and served with lemon wedges and homemade Gooseberry Sauce (see page 99). Try Sautéed Spinach (see page 18) and baked sweet potato as side dishes.

SERVES 3

3 whole mackerel (about ¾ pound each), gutted and cleaned
Juice of ½ lemon
½ cup (1 stick) butter, softened, or corn oil

Salt and freshly ground black pepper
2 tablespoons finely chopped parsley
½ teaspoon finely chopped garlic
2 lemons, cut into wedges

Preheat the broiler.

Wash the mackerel under cold running water and pat dry. Split the mackerel down the center, squeeze lemon juice over the fish, and brush with the softened butter or corn oil. Sprinkle each fish lightly with salt and pepper and place in a buttered or oiled baking dish.

Mix together the parsley and garlic and sprinkle over the top. Place the fish under the broiler and broil for 15 minutes. Serve hot, garnished with the lemon wedges.

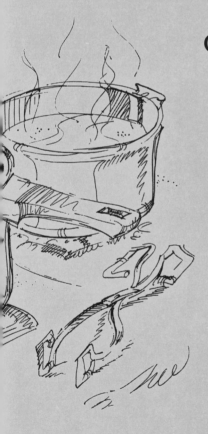

Four

FOR

THE

CUPBOARD

Canned Peaches

Canned Keiffer Pears

Royal Ann Cherries

Pear Chutney

Green Gage Plum Preserves

Spiced Lady Apples

Damson Plum Preserves

Freezing Damson and Other Plums

Wild Berry and Grape Jellies

Wild Strawberry Preserves

Homemade Jelly Bags

Wild Blackberry Jelly

Paraffin

Vidalia Onion Pickles

Cucumber Pickles

Jerusalem Artichoke Pickles

Chestnuts in Heavy Syrup

Pear Chutney

I like to put this chutney on the table when I serve pork or game. It is also delicious made with apples, peaches, or mangoes and will keep for months once made. For the best flavor, use ripe, firm Keiffer pears or another good fall pear. I use a mortar and pestle to crush the chilies, ginger, and garlic because it releases their full flavor and is an easy way to handle these ingredients. The garlic adds wonderful taste to the chutney, which gets better and better as it ages.

MAKES 2 PINTS

1 pound Keiffer pears
Juice of 1 lemon
2 ounces fresh gingerroot
6 dried red chili peppers
2 cups cider vinegar

2 cups sugar
2 tablespoons salt
2 tablespoons mustard seeds
½ pound sultana raisins
10 cloves garlic (about 1 ounce), peeled

Peel and quarter the pears. Slice each pear into about 8 pieces and put them in a bowl. Squeeze the lemon over the pears and let them rest while you prepare the rest of the ingredients.

Bruise the ginger by pounding it in a mortar with a pestle. Take the ginger from the mortar and add the chilies. Crush the chilies in the mortar until well ground. You should have about 3 tablespoons of ground chilies.

Bring the vinegar and sugar to a boil in a large enamel or flameproof glass saucepan. Reduce the heat and simmer for about 10 minutes. Add the ginger, chilies, salt, mustard seeds, raisins, and pear quarters. Bring the syrup back to a boil and then lower the heat and simmer for about 30 minutes, until the chutney thickens.

Crush the garlic cloves in the mortar with the pestle and stir them into the chutney. Let the chutney cool and spoon it into four ½-pint or two 1-pint sterilized jars. Fasten the lids and store in a cool, dark cupboard for at least a month before using. Keep the chutney in the refrigerator after opening. It will keep for a couple of months.

Green Gage Plum Preserves

Although green gage plums have become rare, we still have a few trees in Freetown, planted more than fifty years ago, when nearly everyone had an orchard with a variety of fruit trees. The green gage is a large, lime-colored plum, available in some markets late in August. Eat them fresh, stew them, or make them into preserves.

MAKES 3 TO 4 PINTS

3 pounds green gage plums
1½ pounds sugar
1 lemon, seeded and cut into slices
½ cup water

5-quart stainless steel or enamel
preserving kettle
Four 1-pint jars with lids
Paraffin (see page 194)

Wash and drain the plums. Prick them three or four times with a cake tester or the tip of a sharp knife, and put them in the kettle. Add the sugar, lemon slices, and water, and leave to set for an hour or more.

Mix well and cook over low heat until you see a good amount of liquid at the bottom of the pan. Raise the heat and cook gently for about 45 minutes, until the plums are soft and the syrup is thick. Remove from the heat and set aside until the next day.

Reheat the preserves until hot. Meanwhile sterilize four 1-pint jars and simmer their lids in another small pan. Spoon the preserves into the jars, leaving about ¼ inch of headroom. Wipe the rims clean and pour melted paraffin over the preserves. Let the paraffin cool and fasten the lids securely in place. Set the jars in a cool, dark place until you are ready to use the preserves.

Spiced Lady Apples

This is a quick pickle that can be made the day before or the same day you plan to serve it. When I was young, we always had at least one pickle on the table to serve with meat or game, which may be why we rarely had salad. Lady apples are all over the markets from before Thanksgiving until Christmas. They are rather small, flat apples, just blushed with pink, and look nearly transparent when they are cooked. They're not tart but are lightly sweet and their flavor is enhanced by the spices and sugar in the pickling liquid. I specify Ceylon cinnamon for its very sweet flavor, and I usually buy it at Indian markets or health-food stores.

MAKES ABOUT 2 QUARTS

1 quart cider vinegar

2 pounds granulated sugar

½ pound light brown sugar

3 tablespoons mixed pickling spices

3-inch stick Ceylon cinnamon

5 pounds lady apples

To prepare the syrup: Put the vinegar and sugars into a large, good-quality stainless steel pot. Tie the spices up in a clean piece of cheesecloth and add that to the pot. Stir well, and set the pot on a medium burner. Bring to a simmer and cook gently for 15 minutes.

Wash the apples, leaving the stems on. Prick the surface of the apples in 3 or 4 places to keep the skins from splitting. Put the apples in the vinegar syrup and simmer gently for 30 minutes. When the apples are tender, remove the pot from the heat and let the apples cool in the pot. When cool, put them and the syrup in a large glass jar with a glass clamp-on lid. Store the apples in the refrigerator for 1 to 2 weeks.

Damson Plum Preserves

Sometimes these plums are so full of pectin they do not need quite as much sugar as suggested. They are only in the markets in late August and early September, and even then are hard to find. I buy them from a man with orchards in upstate New York who tells me he has only one very old tree that still produces lots of the small, dark blue plums. Damson plums such as these, from an old variety tree, are very small and very tart; newer strains are a little larger and a little less tart although their flavor is still tangy. I suggest buying damson plums as soon as you see them, since the earlier ones tend to have the most pectin. Take them home and preserve them right away, or freeze them to use later in the winter. Whatever you do, do not give them time to dry out and lose any of their good flavor. The process takes a few days, but is very easy and the results are truly wonderful.

3 pounds blemish-free, firm damson
  plums
2½ pounds sugar

*5-quart stainless steel or enamel
  preserving kettle*
Six to eight 4-ounce jars with lids
Paraffin (see page 194)

Wash the plums well and let them drain dry. Pierce each plum a few times with a cake tester or stout needle and put them in the kettle. Sprinkle the sugar over the plums and leave them overnight.

The next morning, put the kettle holding the sugared plums over medium heat and bring to a simmer. Cook the plums, stirring them gently with a wooden spoon every now and then, until they are tender and the syrup is thick, with a clear plum wine color. To test for doneness, dip a spoon in the syrup and tilt it. If the syrup runs off the spoon in a single drop, the plums are ready to take from the stove. Do not seed the preserves; the seeds add flavor.

Take the kettle from the stove, cover it, and once more leave it overnight. The next morning, heat the preserves until hot and then spoon them into sterilized jars, leaving about ¼ inch headroom. Pour melted paraffin over the preserves and when the paraffin cools and sets, screw the lids on tight. Store the jars in a cool, dry place.

Freezing Damson and Other Plums

Wash the plums and let them dry completely. Lay them in a single layer on a baking sheet and put the sheet in the freezer. After about 20 minutes the plums will be hard enough to pack in clean milk cartons or glass jars for further freezing without the risk of sticking together. When you want to use them, take as many as you need and let them defrost slowly overnight at cool room temperature. If you are making damson plum preserves, pierce the plums when they are completely defrosted and proceed with the recipe.

juice. Learning to recognize these signs on your own is what is so interesting about canning and preserving.

Pour the syrup into the simmering sterilized jars. Fill them not quite to the rim. Leave enough space to hold the paraffin. When the jelly has cooled, wipe the rims of the jars and also the space left for the paraffin; this must be clean in order for the paraffin to adhere to the top of the jelly. Fill the jars with melted paraffin when the jelly is cold. Put the tops on after the paraffin is cold and has set. Label and put the jars in a cool, dry place.

VARIATIONS

Wild grapes are treated in the same manner as blackberries for making jelly. Elderberries and guavas can be prepared in the same way, too, but their juices do not gel very firmly. When you cook guava juice, it will fall from the spoon in a single drop but will not truly gel.

Paraffin

I suggest using paraffin to seal jars holding jams, jellies, and preserves. It's simple to use and really is good protection. You can buy it in the supermarket wherever canning supplies are displayed. For six to eight 8-ounce jars, put about half the cake in a small pan set over hot water to melt. Paraffin is very flammable and so you must take care not to spill any on the open flame. Wipe the rim of the jars clean with a damp cloth and then pour the liquid paraffin over the preserve, filling each jar to the top. Leave the jars uncovered and undisturbed until both the paraffin and preserves are cold. Screw the lids on the jars and store them in a cool, dark closet.

Chestnuts in Heavy Syrup

I love to put up chestnuts in heavy syrup and rum, because they are wonderful to have on hand and I think they are very elegant. They taste so great over vanilla ice cream, or you can just eat them off the spoon.

MAKES TWO PINTS

1 pound large chestnuts

SYRUP

2 cups sugar

1½ cups cold water

½ vanilla bean, split

2 tablespoons rum

To prepare the chestnuts, follow directions in the box on page 278.

Make the syrup by heating the sugar, cold water, and half vanilla bean in a 1-quart saucepan. Bring to a boil and cook briskly for 10 minutes. Add the prepared chestnuts, bring back to a boil, and simmer gently for 12 minutes. In the meantime, sterilize two 1-pint jars by setting them in a pan of water 2 inches deep and simmering them for 10 minutes.

Using a slotted spoon, remove the chestnuts from the syrup and spoon an equal amount into each hot jar. Discard the vanilla bean and boil the syrup briskly for about 15 minutes, until it becomes thick. Skim off any scum that rises to the top. Stir the 2 tablespoons of rum into the hot syrup and pour the syrup over the chestnuts in the jars. Skim any bubbles from the jars and wipe off the rims. Screw on the tops and set the jars in a clean, dry place free of drafts until cold. Then store them in a dark, dry closet.

Five

FROM THE
BREAD OVEN
AND
GRIDDLE

Single-Acting Baking Powder

Benne Seed Biscuits

Biscuits for Two or Three

Buttermilk and Sour Milk

Buttermilk or Sour Milk Biscuits

Cheese Straws

Popovers

Crispy Corn Sticks

Crispy Corn Sticks with Cracklings or Pepper

Saturday Night Yeast Bread

Ethiopian Bread

Cardamom Bread

Hot Yeast Rolls

Orange County Spoon Bread

Corn Batter Cakes

Light Corn Batter Bread

Sourdough Pancakes

Christmas Stollen

Nut Bread

Coffee Cake

WHEN I SET ABOUT MAKING BREAD, the first thing I think of is the flour. While flours today are blended to make standardized all-purpose flours that work pretty well for most cakes, biscuits, breads, and pastries, I still prefer unbleached flour from small mills. Mills such as Byrd Mill in Virginia, Walnut Acres in Pennsylvania, and Arrowhead in Texas grind relatively small quantities of flour to make good, plain unbleached flour. If flour from these mills is unavailable, I buy Hecker's flour (called King Arthur in New England), which is a fine unbleached flour, good for nearly all baking.

When I was young and living in Virginia, we threshed our wheat, took it to the mill, and had it ground into flour for our own use. It came back full of seeds and stones that had to be sifted out before we could bake with it, but that flour really tasted of the wheat berries.

Neighbors would come by during the wheat harvest and help my father in the fields; everyone helped one another out back then, and to get the men off to a good start, my mother often baked biscuits for them. These were white and flaky, just as Southern biscuits ought to be. I make similar biscuits still,

and while I think of them as being part of my heritage, evidently the tender, white biscuits we so quickly associate with the South have only been in existence for about a century.

I remember talking with an old man quite a while ago about the past. The gentleman was 100 years old at the time of our conversation and one of the reasons I found his tales so fascinating was that he had attended school in my grandfather's living room—the first school in the surrounding area after Emancipation. I was interested to learn from him that biscuits used to be considered a food for the well-to-do. Because the technology for refining wheat into pure white flour was quite new back then, only the rich could afford the new, bleached-out flour, and even then cakes and biscuits made with it were considered very special indeed. Black cooks who could make light, tender biscuits were in demand and so the recipes and techniques passed from one generation to another.

Bleached flour may have been popular in the last century, but I have never been sure why flour manufacturers have continued to make it, unless it keeps better on the shelf. I do not like to use it because of the chemicals needed to bleach it. And, of course, nowadays we have discovered that whole wheat flour is healthier and tastes good, too, and so we use it to make all sorts of breads (if not biscuits).

Although I love their taste, over the years I have grown weary of the time it takes to make traditional yeast breads and so have developed some recipes that do not require kneading. I also make a lot of batter breads, spoon bread, and hot breads such as popovers. I suppose there are as many ways to make batter breads, such as corn bread, as there are cooks who make them. Everyone measures slightly differently and mixes the batter a little more or a little less than someone else. Whatever way they are made, batter breads and spoon breads taste best when they are eaten fresh from the oven and still warm, which is why I always try to make them at the last minute when I am preparing a meal. I have never thought corn bread tasted very good heated up the next day.

I feel the same way about hot griddle cakes. You can mix up the batter ahead of time, but once the cakes are cooked, they should be lifted straight off the griddle and onto a warm plate, and then spread with sweet butter and syrup or preserves. Such freshness is possible only at home, which is why these quick breads and hot cakes never taste quite the same in restaurants.

The South has long been famous for its great hot breads and pancakes. I think the rich buttermilk or naturally soured milk, home rendered lard, and

single-acting baking powder Southern cooks always baked with have given our breads this deserved reputation. As I discuss in this chapter, I feel strongly about single-acting baking powder and buttermilk. I object to the chemical taste of double-acting baking powder and I know if you ever try real buttermilk, you will not be satisfied with the cultured type sold in most supermarkets. Lard, by the way, is discussed in the chapter on desserts.

There are a number of bakeries that make very good breads, particularly yeast breads. If you are fortunate enough to have a good bakery nearby, buy bread from it when you cannot make it yourself. Bread, to me, should be part of every meal. It is so good, so satisfying, and, if you take a bit of time, not at all difficult to make yourself.

SINGLE-ACTING BAKING POWDER

It has been my experience that double-acting baking powder has a bitter after-taste, which is why I prefer single-acting baking powder that I make myself. I make a pound at a time and the baking powder keeps for three or four weeks without any loss of strength. You do not have to make as much as I do, but if you do make it, I think you will notice a difference in flavor. I recommend that you weigh the ingredients when measuring them out, but if you use measuring spoons and cups, use a light hand and do not pack them down. Also, it just isn't true that when you use single-acting baking powder you have to mix up the dry and liquid ingredients quickly and bake them right away or else the batter will die. I make spoon bread batter the night before and it rises just fine the next day.

MAKES ABOUT 1 CUP

2 ounces (¼ cup) cream of tartar
1 ounce (2 tablespoons) baking soda

1½ ounces (3 tablespoons) cornstarch

Mix as much as you need following this ratio and weighing the ingredients. Store the baking powder in a glass jar with a lid; it will keep for a month or more.

BENNE SEED BISCUITS

Benne seeds, which are also known as sesame seeds, were brought to America long ago with the Africans. Their name derives from the Benue State of Nigeria. The Nigerian name for this seed is *beni*. Slaves planted them at the ends of crop rows and around their small cabins and used them in much of their cooking. They are still extremely popular in the South and turn up in recipes for cereals, breads, cookies, and biscuits. I think their flavor is best when they are toasted, and short of burning them, the longer you toast them, the better they are. These crisp little biscuits go well with cocktails, pâtés, and soups, or anytime you would want a cracker.

1 cup benne seeds	1 teaspoon salt
3 cups flour	⅔ cup lard
1½ teaspoons single-acting baking	⅔ cup milk
powder (see page 208)	Salt

Preheat the oven to 425°F.

Put the benne seeds in a shallow pan in the preheated oven. Look at them after 5 minutes to check on the color—they should be the color of butterscotch and they should have a delicious toasted smell. If not ready, shake the pan and return them to the oven for 1 to 2 minutes—but *watch carefully.*

Sift the flour, baking powder, and salt into a large bowl. Add the lard and work the mixture with a pastry blender or your fingertips until it has the texture of cornmeal. Add the milk and mix well. Mix in the benne seeds. Place the dough on a floured surface, knead for a few seconds, and shape into a ball. Roll the dough out until it is about the thickness of a nickel. Using a 2-inch biscuit cutter, stamp out rounds and lay them on an ungreased baking sheet or a baking sheet lined with parchment paper. Bake for about 12 minutes, until lightly browned. Remove from the oven, sprinkle with a little bit of salt, and serve hot. You may store the cooled biscuits in an airtight tin or jar and reheat them before serving.

BISCUITS FOR TWO OR THREE

I used to make biscuits for at least 5 or 6 people, but since I have been living alone, I have altered my biscuit recipe to make 8 or 10 large biscuits that are just the way I want them. The recipe is quick and you do not have leftovers, which never taste as good as freshly baked biscuits. I like my biscuits large and use an upturned glass or empty 2½-inch-round tin can to stamp them out. If I know I will be making these or any other biscuits, I measure everything out beforehand and then all I have to do is mix the dough and bake the biscuits.

MAKES 8 TO 10 BISCUITS

½ pound unbleached all-purpose flour

½ teaspoon salt

4 teaspoons single-acting baking
   powder (see page 208)

2 ounces chilled lard

⅔ cup milk

Put the flour, salt, baking powder, and lard in a mixing bowl. Blend with a pastry blender or with your fingertips until the mixture is the texture of corn-meal. Add the milk all at once and stir the mixture well with a stout spoon. Scrape the dough out of the bowl onto a lightly floured surface. Sprinkle the dough lightly with 1 teaspoon of flour to prevent its sticking to your fingers. Knead the dough for a few seconds and shape it into a round, thick cake. Dust the rolling surface and the rolling pin again lightly with flour, and roll the dough from the center outward into a circle. Lift up the dough and turn it as you roll to make a circle 9 inches in diameter. Pierce the dough all over with a dinner fork and cut with a biscuit cutter, beginning on the outer edge and cutting in as close as possible to avoid too much leftover dough. This will yield 8 to 10 large biscuits. Place on a heavy cookie sheet or baking pan. Bake in preheated 450°F oven for 12 to 13 minutes. Remove from the oven and allow to cool for 3 or 4 minutes before serving. Serve hot. Biscuits can be warmed over successfully if set uncovered in a hot oven for no more than 4 to 5 minutes.

Buttermilk and Sour Milk

When I can get it, I like to use buttermilk in biscuits. Buttermilk is the liquid that separates from solid butter during the butter-making process, and although plenty of butter is made today, real buttermilk is hard to come by. The buttermilk sold in supermarkets is cultured skim milk, which I don't think adds very good flavor to biscuits, pancakes, or anything else. If I want a tangy flavor and do not have buttermilk, I sour some milk myself by adding a tablespoon of cider vinegar to sweet milk for every cup or so called for in the recipe.

Buttermilk or Sour Milk Biscuits

It is the buttermilk or sour milk that gives these biscuits a slightly sharp flavor that is different from biscuits made with sweet milk. When making biscuits, be sure to measure all the ingredients carefully. The right balance makes the difference between dry or heavy biscuits and biscuits that are just right. I also think lard is important as it produces nice, light biscuits. The dough should not be too wet or too dry; the correct consistency is moist and almost sticky. If the dough is dry, the biscuit will be dry; if it is too wet, the biscuit will be heavy. Another reason for leaden biscuits is too little kneading. You should not knead the dough for more than a few seconds, but the kneading has to be very intense. Cut biscuits out with anything—a biscuit or cookie cutter, a glass, anything round—but be careful not to twist the cutter as you lift it from the dough—just press down and pull straight up.

45 TO 50 2-INCH BISCUITS

1 pound unbleached all-purpose flour

2 teaspoons salt

2 tablespoons single-acting baking powder (see page 208)

4 ounces chilled lard, cut into pieces (see page 260)

1 cup plus 2 tablespoons buttermilk

Preheat oven to 450°F.

Mix together the flour, salt, and baking powder in a large mixing bowl. Mix well. Add the chilled lard and blend quickly with a pastry blender or your fingertips until the mixture becomes the texture of cornmeal. Add the milk all at once, then stir vigorously for a few seconds with a stout wooden spoon. Work the dough into a ball and turn onto a lightly floured surface. Knead the dough vigorously for 3 seconds, then shape the dough into a round cake. Dust the rolling pin and rolling surface lightly with flour. Roll the dough evenly from the center outward into a ¼-inch thickness. Pierce the surface of the dough with a dinner fork, then cut out biscuits using a 2½-inch biscuit cutter dipped in flour. For nice, straight-sided biscuits do not wiggle the cutter. Press straight down and pull up sharply. I find it is best to start with the outer edge of the circle. Cut very close to the edge so as to waste as little of the dough as possible. Leftover dough does not make pretty biscuits. The texture is also affected by rerolling. Place biscuits ¼ inch apart on a heavy cookie sheet with a shiny surface. Otherwise, put biscuits on a piece of aluminum foil with the shiny side up. Biscuits will brown better if they are baked on a shiny surface. Bake in a preheated 450°F oven for 12 to 13 minutes. Remove the biscuits from the oven. Leave for a few minutes, then serve hot. Biscuits can be reheated by setting them in a 375°F oven on a baking sheet, uncovered, for 4 to 5 minutes.

Cheese Straws

Cheese straws are common throughout the South, served with cocktails, soups, sandwiches, and salads. I like to make mine very peppery and use a good extra-sharp cheese for flavor. The straws are not yeast raised and when they're baked, they are flat and very crisp. I often freeze the dough so all I have to do is cut off what I need as I want it.

MAKES ABOUT 4 DOZEN

1⅔ cups flour
1 teaspoon salt
½ cup (1 stick) butter
¼ teaspoon cayenne

7 ounces sharp cheddar cheese, finely grated
1 large egg, beaten
2 tablespoons water

Put the flour, salt, butter, and cayenne in a 2-quart mixing bowl. Blend well until the texture is that of cornmeal. Add the grated cheese, and blend in well. Add the egg plus the water and mix well with a mixer or by hand, until the dough is free of dots of cheese. Knead the dough into a ball or flat cake. Let rest for 15 minutes. Wrap in wax paper and refrigerate until ready to roll out. Roll the dough out ⅛ inch thick. Cut into strips ¼ inch wide and 4 inches in length. Cook in a preheated 400°F oven for about 25 minutes, until golden and crisp. Remove and serve hot.

POPOVERS

Popovers are another Southern bread that can be served with any meal, but which I particularly like for breakfast with maple syrup. For lunch they are good with soups or cheese soufflé, and later in the afternoon with honey butter and a cup of tea or coffee when friends drop by. Popovers are easy to make and I find that when I put them in a basket with other muffins and breads, they are the first to go. You may mix the batter the night before but if you do not, let it rest for at least an hour before baking or the popovers will not puff up. It is also important to serve them right away while they are piping hot. The only trick to baking them is not to open the oven door for 20 minutes—they need the time to expand until there is nothing left inside. When done, they look like big mushrooms.

12 POPOVERS

2 cups sifted unbleached all-purpose
  flour (measured after sifting)
½ teaspoon salt
3 eggs
2 cups milk
Unsalted butter

*Two 6-cup muffin tins or twelve 4-ounce
  Pyrex cups*

(recipe continues)

Preheat the oven to 375°F.

Put the flour and salt in a mixing bowl and mix well. Beat the eggs lightly with a fork. Pour the milk into the eggs and mix well. Now pour the milk mixture slowly into the flour, stirring constantly. Cover lightly with a cloth and let rest for an hour or more before baking. Lightly grease 12 muffins tins or Pyrex cups with unsalted butter. Heat the pans or cups hot without burning the butter, and then pour in ⅓ cup of batter. Set the filled pans in the preheated oven for 25 minutes. Do not open the oven for 20 minutes. Otherwise, the popovers will collapse and be ruined. To obtain hollow, dry popovers, this rule has to be observed. They should be perfectly baked in 25 minutes. Serve hot from the oven.

NOTE:
½ cup of whole wheat flour can be substituted for the same amount of white flour.

CRISPY CORN STICKS

For my taste, most corn sticks are too thick. This is because they are baked in molded pans specially designed for them that I think are too big. Until someone comes up with a better pan, I will continue to bake corn sticks in pleated aluminum foil set in a baking pan. Baked this way, they are crispy and thin, good with hot or cold soups and as part of a bread basket or hors d'oeuvres tray. I cut strong foil to a length of 18 inches and a width of 6 inches, butter it with sweet butter, and pleat it to make 18 troughs, each about ½ inch deep and ½ inch wide. I run my middle finger down the center of each trough to round it out, more or less, and leave the ends open. The foil fits on a baking sheet and no batter runs out of the filled troughs. When I make this batter, I have found it is a good idea to loosen the cornmeal and flour a little by stirring them lightly before spooning them into the measuring cup.

MAKES 18 CORN STICKS

1 cup water-ground cornmeal

2 tablespoons unbleached all-purpose
  flour

½ cup milk

3 tablespoons melted butter

1 teaspoon salt

1 teaspoon sugar

3 teaspoons single-acting baking
  powder (see page 208)

1 egg

Put the cornmeal and flour in a large mixing bowl. Heat the milk to boiling and immediately pour it over the cornmeal and flour, stirring as you do so. Add the melted butter, mix well, and set the batter aside to cool completely.

Preheat the oven to 450°F.

(recipe continues)

Stir the salt, sugar, and baking powder into the cool batter. When they are well mixed, add the egg and mix well again. Spoon the batter into the aluminum foil troughs that you have prepared as described. Use a knife to neaten up the edges of the troughs so that no batter is spilling over the sides.

Put the baking tray in the oven and immediately lower the temperature to 375°F. Bake for 13 to 18 minutes, until golden brown. Remove the baking tray from the oven and lift the foil from the pan. Pull the sides of the foil out at once: the sticks will fall into the center of the foil. Serve while still hot.

CRISPY CORN STICKS WITH CRACKLINGS OR PEPPER

Add ⅓ cup cracklings, cut into ¼-inch cubes, to the batter. Or stir ¼ teaspoon coarsely ground fresh black pepper into the batter.

SATURDAY NIGHT YEAST BREAD

We always began making yeast bread on Saturday night and baked it on Sunday. We had made the yeast from cornmeal and let it ferment and dry out before cutting it into cakes. We would use the yeast to make the sponge for the bread and then mix the dough and let it rise overnight. We'd then push it down Sunday morning and let it rise again before baking it for breakfast. I love yeast bread but I don't always have time for doughs that require long kneading, so over the years I have developed recipes that require a little less work than the breads I made as a child. For one thing, you no longer have to make yeast but can buy good yeast without preservatives in supermarkets.

This yeast bread requires no kneading. Proper rising is most important here and I suggest setting the dough over a pan of hot water to rise, especially if your kitchen is cooler than 80°F. Summer is the best time for yeast breads because it is so warm and moist. The bread has to rise twice, and then again in the oven. I have always started with a sponge and I think it helps rise the bread properly. Before the second rising, I roll the dough with my hands to shape it into loaves, and as I roll it, I coat it with a thin layer of flour. The flour makes the crust crispy but the loaves do not look white when done, as some flour-coated breads do.

MAKES 4 LOAVES

3 cups unbleached all-purpose flour	½ cup milk
1 tablespoon sugar	1¼ cups water
1 teaspoon salt	4 teaspoons lard
1 package active dry yeast	1 cup whole wheat flour

To make the sponge, put 1 cup of white flour in a large mixing bowl. Add the sugar, salt, and yeast, and mix well. Scald the milk, cool it with ½ cup of water, and add to the flour mixture. Stir lightly and set the bowl in a warm (80° to 90°F) draft-free place to rise for 25 minutes. Meanwhile, heat the lard with the remaining ¾ cup water until melted, and set aside to cool until the sponge is ready.

Combine the remaining 2 cups of white flour with the whole wheat flour in a large bowl. When the yeast sponge is ready (it should be light and bub-

(recipe continues)

bly), stir it into the flour. Add the water and lard mixture and stir well. Cover the bowl with a cloth and return the dough to a warm spot to rise. When it is doubled in size, gently push it down and let it rise until doubled in volume once more.

Turn the dough onto a floured surface, shape it and smooth it over, and divide it into 4 equal parts. Take each piece of dough and roll into a sausage-like shape on a lightly floured surface. This is done by rolling with both hands open, and pushing away as you press until the dough is the proper shape and length (about 5 inches or longer). Keep the surface floured to help achieve a crusty surface on the bread. Place the loaves side by side, about 2 inches apart, to rise on a heavy cookie sheet. Put the loaves to rise in the same warm spot as before. When fully risen (25 to 30 minutes) they will be light to the touch and doubled in volume.

Preheat the oven to 425°F.

Make four incisions about ½ inch deep across the top of each loaf with a sharp, clean razor blade. Bake the loaves in the preheated oven for 25 minutes. Remove from the oven and place on wire racks to cool before serving.

ETHIOPIAN BREAD

While certainly not a Southern bread, this has become one of my favorites. The turmeric gives it an unusual taste—one of those flavors you just want to keep eating. When I visit my Ethiopian friends who taught me this recipe, I am served the bread with coffee while I wait for the big meal they always fix for me. These women, who are sisters studying in the United States and who call me their mother in America, make the bread in a roasting pan with a cover. It browns nicely and is soft, not crusty.

MAKES TWO 8-INCH LOAVES

1 package active dry yeast	½ cup vegetable oil
2 cups lukewarm water	1 teaspoon salt
6 to 7 cups unbleached all-purpose flour	1 teaspoon black caraway seeds
	2 teaspoons turmeric

Dissolve the yeast in ¼ cup of the water. Put 6 cups of the flour in a large bowl. Add the oil, salt, caraway seeds, and turmeric. Stir in the remaining water and the dissolved yeast. Turn out onto a floured surface and knead, adding more flour as necessary, until smooth.

Put the dough in a lightly greased bowl, cover, and leave to rise in a warm place for 3 to 4 hours, until doubled in volume. Punch down and form into 2 loaves. Place in 2 greased 8-inch loaf pans, cover, and let rise again until doubled in volume.

Preheat the oven to 375°F.

Bake the loaves in the preheated oven for 1 hour, covering each loaf with a baking pan of the same size. Remove from the pans and cool on racks. When cold, wrap in wax paper and store in a cool place.

CARDAMOM BREAD

I was taken with the taste of this bread from the first bite. It is a bread of Swedish origin with a light texture and delicious slightly sweet flavor. Making it is not too different from making yeast rolls.

MAKES 2 BRAIDED LOAVES

1 package active dry yeast

⅓ cup lukewarm milk

1 egg, lightly beaten

¼ cup sugar

1 teaspoon salt

1 teaspoon crushed cardamom seeds

⅓ cup melted butter

2 cups sifted unbleached all-purpose flour

1 tablespoon melted butter (for brushing loaves)

½ cup sugar cubes, crushed

Sprinkle the yeast over the milk in a large bowl. Stir well and then add the egg, sugar, salt, cardamom, and ⅓ cup melted butter. Mix thoroughly and add the flour. Stir until the dough is well mixed and then turn it out onto a lightly floured work surface.

Knead the dough for about 5 minutes and form it into a rounded piece. Brush it lightly with the tablespoon of melted butter and put it back in the bowl. Cover loosely and set the bowl in a warm, draft-free place to rise and

double in bulk. This will take about 1½ hours. Push the dough down and let it rise again in the bowl until nearly doubled.

Preheat the oven to 375°F.

Take the dough from the bowl and put it on a lightly floured surface. Divide the dough into 2 pieces and then separate each piece into 3 smaller pieces so that you have 6 pieces in all. Roll each piece of dough into sausage-shaped strands of equal length. Take 3 strands and, after pressing them together at one end, braid them. Repeat with the 3 remaining pieces of dough so you have 2 braided loaves. Lay the loaves in a buttered 8-by-8-by-2-inch baking pan and brush lightly with melted butter. Sprinkle crushed sugar cubes over the tops of the loaves, let rise to the top of the pan, and bake them for 30 minutes.

NOTE:
To crush sugar cubes, wrap them in a clean cloth and pound them with a mallet until roughly crushed—there should still be some small lumps.

HOT YEAST ROLLS

As we know, Southerners love their hot breads, and yeast rolls such as these are no exception. Since you can mix the dough the night before and leave it in the refrigerator, these rolls are good when you are planning a big meal. As with all yeast breads, good rising times are the most important aspect of making the yeast rolls. This dough requires no kneading.

MAKES ABOUT 24 ROLLS

1 tablespoon lard

1 tablespoon butter

1⅓ cups hot water

4 cups sifted unbleached all-purpose flour

1 package active dry yeast

2 tablespoons sugar

1 teaspoon salt

1 egg, lightly beaten

⅔ cup melted butter

Put the lard and butter in a small bowl and pour the hot water over them. Set aside and cool to lukewarm.

Combine the flour, yeast, sugar, and salt in a large, deep bowl and mix well. Add the lard and butter mixture and the egg and stir until well blended. Cover and leave in the refrigerator overnight.

The next day, take the bowl from the refrigerator and put it in a warm place to rise, loosely covered with a clean towel. Depending on the warmth of the room, the dough will double in bulk in 2 to 4 hours.

Preheat the oven to 375°F.

Pinch off pieces of dough and form into 24 small rolls. Arrange the rolls in a 9-by-9-by-2-inch baking pan and brush each one with melted butter. Leave the rolls to rise, loosely covered, until they reach the top of the pan, about an hour. Bake for 35 to 40 minutes, until browned, and serve hot.

ORANGE COUNTY SPOON BREAD

Spoon bread has long been one of the South's most popular breads. Since I was a child growing up in Orange County, Virginia, I have loved it. This recipe makes a bread that has a somewhat lighter texture than other spoon breads because it contains grated fresh corn blended to a liquid state. Since I prefer not to use flour in spoon bread, I use the fresh corn to help keep the batter from separating. And as good as it is for a binding agent, it is even better as a flavoring agent. Serve spoon bread, which is meant to be spooned out of the serving dish, with foods that have a nice sauce for the bread.

SERVES 4

1 cup corn, freshly cut from about 4 ears of corn
2½ cups milk
3 whole eggs
3 tablespoons melted butter
¾ cup white cornmeal
1 teaspoon sugar
1 teaspoon salt
2 tablespoons single-acting baking powder
   (see page 208)

Preheat the oven to 375°F.

Put the corn in a blender or food processor. Add the milk and blend just long enough to liquefy. Add the remaining ingredients and blend.

Pour the batter into a hot, buttered 1-quart loaf pan or soufflé dish. You can also use individual soufflé dishes if you prefer. Bake the spoon bread at 375°F for about 25 minutes, or until the bread has set in the center. If you bake it in individual soufflé dishes, which are usually about 4 ounces, bake the spoon bread for about 10 to 12 minutes. Serve immediately.

CORN BATTER CAKES

Cornmeal gives these griddle cakes a stronger, tangier flavor than pancakes made with wheat flour. Leaving the batter to sit overnight or longer helps develop the deliciously sour flavor even more. These corn cakes are best with Southern syrups such as Louisiana cane syrup and sorghum molasses. You could use maple syrup, although I rarely do since we don't make it in the South.

When you cook these or any other griddle cakes, let the griddle get very hot. Grease it with just a little lard—butter will burn—and after you get into cooking you will not have to add any more lard as the griddle will be well seasoned. Some cornmeals are more coarsely ground than others and I prefer finely ground meal. I have found Byrd Mill White Water Ground, Indian Head White Water Ground, and Lindley Mill are good brands. I understand some people suggest mixing wheat flour with cornmeal to make a finer mixture, but I do not recommend it since you lose the full flavor of the corn.

MAKES 12 TO 16 GRIDDLE CAKES

1 cup white cornmeal	2 eggs
Scant ½ teaspoon salt	⅔ cup milk, at room temperature
2 teaspoons single-acting baking powder (see page 208)	2 teaspoons melted butter
	½ teaspoon baking soda (optional)

Put the cornmeal, salt, and baking powder in a mixing bowl. Beat the eggs in a separate bowl, pour in milk, and mix well. Stir the milk and eggs into the meal mixture and mix thoroughly. Cover the bowl and set the batter in the refrigerator overnight or a little longer.

Before making the cakes, remove the batter from the refrigerator and allow it to return to room temperature. Mix well. Just before cooking, stir in the melted butter. Spoon the batter onto a hot, greased griddle to make pancakes. Turn the cakes when bubbles appear on the top and cook the other side for 4 to 5 seconds. These cakes should be very thin. If the batter gets too thick, add a tablespoon or two of milk and stir well again. If the pancakes separate when cooking, add the optional baking soda to the batter and mix well. The batter will sometimes separate if it becomes very fermented.

LIGHT CORN BATTER BREAD

Each batter bread is a little bit different from the next, but they are all similar, too. They say there are as many ways to make batter breads as there are cooks baking them. One day I went to make corn batter bread and had no milk. I had heavy cream, though, and so I added water to it to thin it and I ended up with the lightest batter bread I had ever baked. The texture is soft but not as liquid as spoon bread.

MAKES 16 SQUARES

1 tablespoon butter

1 large egg

1¼ cups cold water

½ teaspoon salt

1 scant teaspoon sugar

1 tablespoon single-acting baking powder (see page 208)

1 tablespoon flour

1 cup water-ground white cornmeal

1 cup heavy cream

Preheat oven to 375°F.

Grease a 9-by-9-by-2- or 8-by-8-by-1-inch baking pan with the butter and put it in the oven to warm for 4 minutes.

The next seven ingredients can be put into a blender for three seconds at the liquefying speed. Pour the batter into a bowl and add the heavy cream, which should not go in the blender as it tends to turn to butter. Stir well with a spoon and pour the mixture into the hot greased baking pan.

Bake for 25 minutes. Remove from the oven and let rest for about 20 minutes. Cut into squares and serve hot.

Sourdough Pancakes

I have always made sourdough starter by fermenting flour, yeast, and water for 8 to 10 hours—enough time for the flavor to develop. Even so, I think the flavor is helped almost as much by bottled water that has no chemicals to interfere with the batter. The yeast in the starter makes the pancakes rise up during cooking but they are not as thick and cakey as some. Since this batter and the batter for Corn Batter Cakes can be made ahead, I make both and enjoy the two flavors during a leisurely weekend breakfast. Try these with honey butter, guava jelly, stewed blueberries, or raspberry jam.

MAKES 24 PANCAKES

STARTER

1½ cups unbleached all-purpose flour   1 cup bottled lukewarm water
1½ teaspoons active dry yeast

PANCAKE BATTER

1 cup milk, at room temperature   1 teaspoon baking soda
1 egg, beaten   2 teaspoons melted butter
½ teaspoon salt   Lard, for greasing the griddle
1 teaspoon sugar

To make the starter: In a 1½-quart bowl, mix the flour and yeast. Slowly add the water, stirring until well mixed. Cover lightly and leave out in the kitchen overnight—8 to 10 hours.

To make the batter: Mix the milk, beaten egg, salt, sugar, baking soda, and melted butter together thoroughly, then combine with the starter. Spoon about ¼ cup of batter onto a hot buttered griddle to cook until the cake is dotted over with little bubbles. Then turn over and cook another 2 to 3 minutes. Serve hot with desired syrups.

CHRISTMAS STOLLEN

This is one of my favorite Christmas sweet breads. I like traditional fruitcake, too, but have not made it in a couple of years. But I *always* make stollen. It is light and not overly sweet. To make it right you should use bitter almonds, which are hard to find. I learned from a German friend that another secret is to press the almonds and fruit into the dough after sprinkling them over the surface, rather than stirring them into the dough. When they are pressed into the dough, you fold the dough up like a baby wrapped in swaddling clothes. As with other fruitcakes, you can make stollen months before the holiday rush, which is helpful since making it is a big job. You can also make it in the middle of December and let it sit for only a couple of weeks. Be sure to start the vanilla sugar 1 week to 1 month ahead. I usually prepare a big stollen well ahead of time, one twice the size of this one. I bake it on a sheet pan and then brush it with a pound of melted butter and let the butter soak in. Next, I sprinkle lots of confectioners' sugar over it until it looks like snow. I wrap it real tight in parchment and then foil, and leave it in a cool cupboard and just forget about it. At Christmastime I cut it into pieces to give to my friends.

MAKES 1 VERY LARGE STOLLEN

VANILLA SUGAR

- 1 box confectioners' sugar
- 1 vanilla bean

- 5 packages (4½ tablespoons) active dry yeast
- 9 cups unbleached all-purpose flour
- ⅔ cup superfine sugar
- 1½ cups warm milk
- Scant teaspoon salt

- 3 cups (6 sticks) unsalted butter, at room temperature
- Grated rind of 2 lemons
- ⅓ cup Jamaican rum
- 4 ounces sweet almonds in the skin
- ⅓ ounce bitter almonds in the skin
- ¾ cup (6 ounces) citron
- 2½ cups seedless raisins
- ¾ cup (6 ounces) currants

Prepare the vanilla sugar at least a week, or even a month, before you make the stollen. Fill a 1-quart glass jar with the confectioners' sugar and stick the vanilla bean in the center. Put the lid on tight and store in the cupboard.

Put the yeast, 1 cup of the flour, 2 tablespoons of the superfine sugar, and

(recipe continues)

the warm milk in a bowl. Let it sit for about 20 minutes or so, until the mixture becomes foamy and bubbly. Stir in the remaining flour and sugar and add the salt and 2 cups of unsalted butter. Because this is such a heavy and unwieldy dough, don't attempt to blend these ingredients with a spoon. Turn the dough onto a board and knead with a rocking motion for about 30 minutes, turning the dough from time to time, folding it over on itself. You may knead the dough in a heavy-duty mixer with a dough hook. Add the grated lemon rind and sprinkle on the rum, a little at a time. Knead for a few minutes more, until they are well blended. Cover the dough and let it sit in a warm spot to rise for 2 to 3 hours, until doubled.

While the dough is rising, chop the nuts and cut the citron slices into small pieces. Turn out the dough on a board. Knead it into a wide circle about 18 inches across and ½ inch thick. Sprinkle with the nuts, raisins, currants, and citron. Press them into the dough and knead until they are evenly distributed. Fold the dough in half and knead it back into an 18-inch circle. Again, fold the dough over this time to within 1½ inches of the lower half and round off the top edge with your hand. Slide the dough onto a heavy cookie sheet, cover, and let rise another 30 minutes in a warm spot. Place a 10-inch pie plate on the bottom of the oven and pour in 2 cups of boiling water. Preheat the oven to 375°F and set the stollen on the middle rack to bake for 1¾ hours. Remove the pan of water after 45 minutes and reduce the temperature to 325°F. Look to make sure the stollen is not getting too brown. If it is, cover loosely with brown paper. Remove from the oven after it has baked for the full time, and with two wide spatulas, lift it onto a rack to cool. When it is just lukewarm, brush with the remaining cup of butter. Let stand for about 5 minutes or more. Then sift the vanilla sugar over the top to make a good coating, about ½ inch deep. Remember to store the stollen in a tightly covered tin or wrap it in heavy wax paper with an outer wrap of foil. Stollen keeps well for three weeks to a month.

NUT BREAD

We don't see nut bread too much today but there is something about this old-fashioned bread that is so good. It is not too sweet and goes well with either tea or coffee. One day when I was playing around with the texture of the bread I added millet meal. Now I always use it, as well as white flour and whole wheat flour. The combination gives the bread body as well as wholesome flavor. You can find millet meal in health-food stores and even some supermarkets. Do not confuse it with millet flour, which is not as coarse. I find that this bread tastes best if I let the batter rest for a few minutes before baking. I guess it gives the flavors time to blend.

MAKES 2 SMALL LOAVES, OR 1 LARGE ONE

3 cups unbleached all-purpose flour
½ cup whole wheat flour
½ cup millet meal
⅓ cup brown sugar
1 tablespoon granulated sugar
1 teaspoon salt
3 teaspoons single-acting baking powder (see page 208)
½ teaspoon vanilla
1 large egg
1 cup milk
1 cup chopped fresh walnuts, not too fine

Preheat oven to 350°F.

Put the flours, millet meal, sugars, salt, baking powder, and vanilla in a large bowl. Beat the egg thoroughly, stir in the milk, and pour this into the flour mixture. Mix well and add the walnuts. Mix well again. Grease 2 small loaf pans (or use 1 large 9¾-by-5¾-inch pan). Spoon an equal amount of the batter into each pan—they should be three-quarters full. Let them rest for at least 25 minutes before placing them in the oven to bake for 45 minutes. If the batter is baked in a single loaf, the baking time will be 1 hour. Remove from the oven, turn the loaves onto a cake rack, and cool. When cold, wrap the bread in wax paper. Store in a cool, dry place, not in the refrigerator.

COFFEE CAKE

This coffee cake is rich but has a light texture. I think of it more as a brunch cake than a breakfast bread, and although it "takes a lot doing" to make it, it's worth it.

SERVES 8 TO 10

4 teaspoons active dry yeast	½ cup lukewarm milk
1 teaspoon salt	4 eggs plus 1 egg yolk, lightly beaten
2 cups unbleached all-purpose flour	⅔ cup very soft unsalted butter

FILLING

2 teaspoons cinnamon	⅔ cup chopped walnuts
⅔ cup superfine sugar	⅔ cup seedless raisins, cut in half
2 egg whites, beaten to soft peaks	1 tablespoon melted butter
1 cup raspberry preserves	

Mix together the yeast, salt, and 3 tablespoons of the flour in a deep mixing bowl. Stir in the milk. Set the bowl in a warm, draft-free place for 15 to 20 minutes, until the mixture becomes bubbly. Add the eggs and the remainder of the flour, mixing well until the batter is smooth. Add the softened butter and stir for about 5 minutes, until the dough is smooth and elastic. Turn the dough into a shallow bowl, cover loosely, and chill in the refrigerator overnight.

To prepare the filling: Mix together the cinnamon and sugar. Have the beaten egg whites, preserves, and chopped nuts and raisins at hand. Spread out 2 sheets of wax paper, about 22 inches long, so that the sheet nearest you overlaps the second sheet by several inches. Dust both generously with flour (about ½ cup). Work swiftly with the dough as it is very fragile. With a cake spatula, pry the dough out of the dish in which it was chilled. Turn it onto the floured wax paper and start to roll it out, using a chilled rolling pin well dusted with flour. After each roll, pick up the dough and give it a quarter turn. If it begins to stick, dust the sticky spot with flour. Roll the dough out into a rectangular shape, about 18 by 12 inches and ¼ inch or more thick.

Brush the beaten egg whites over the dough to within 2 inches of the edges. Quickly sprinkle the nuts, raisins, cinnamon sugar, and 10 to 12 teaspoons of raspberry preserves over the dough. Now roll the dough up in jelly-roll fashion. To do this, lift up the edge of the wax paper closest to you and give it a quick flip away from you to start the dough rolling. Turn the dough about 3 times and then flip the far edge of the paper toward you to finish the roll. Grasping each end of the paper, lift the rolled dough, bend it gently into a horseshoe, and slide it into a 10-inch tube pan, 3 inches deep. Join the ends of the horseshoe by tilting the pan and shaking it gently. With a rubber spatula, lightly press down the dough so that the ring settles evenly on the bottom of the pan. Brush the dough ring with the melted butter. Put the pan in a warm, draft-free place (about 80°F), cover loosely with a cloth, and leave until the dough has risen to within an inch of the top of the pan.

Preheat the oven to 375°F for 15 minutes, and bake the cake for 45 minutes. Remove from the oven and set the pan on a wire rack to cool for about 12 minutes before turning out onto a serving plate.

Six

THE
GOOD TASTE
OF
OLD-FASHIONED
DESSERTS

Summer Pudding

Old-fashioned Custard-based Vanilla Ice Cream

Green Gage Plum Ice Cream

Ultra-Pasteurized Cream

Caramel Sauce for Ice Cream

Damson Plum Sauce for Ice Cream

Cranberry Sauce with Rum

Raspberry Sherbet

Tangerine Sherbet

Fresh Peach Cobbler

Nutmeg Sauce

Freezing Blackberries, Blueberries, Raspberries, Gooseberries, and Currants

Blackberry Roly-poly

Pie Plates

Raspberry Pie Garnished with Whipped Cream

Pastry Shells

Lard Pie Pastry

Lard

Blackberry or Boysenberry Pie

Red Currant Pie

Wild Persimmon Tarts

Tyler Pie

Damson Plum Pie

Mincemeat Tarts with Brandy Butter

Marinated Apple Tart with Custard Sauce

Poached Pears

Apple Brown Betty

Baked Staymen Winesap Apples with
Rich Custard Sauce

Chestnuts with Chocolate Glaze

Chestnuts

Pralines

Pralines for Sprinkling

Chocolate Soufflé

Orange Soufflé with Orange Sauce

Coconut Layer Cake with Lemon Filling

Chocolate Iced Layer Cake

Small Cakes

Black Walnut Pound Cake

Whiskey Cake

Meringue Shells

Rich Floating Island with Raspberry Preserves
and Spun Sugar

Spun Sugar

Plum Pudding

Baking Cookies

Nut Butter Balls

Special Sugar Cookies for Decorating

Butter Cookies

MOST OF THE DESSERTS in this chapter are very simple—the sort of desserts we had when I was a child growing up in the country. In those days, we sat down for every meal and although during planting and harvest we often had no time for dessert (there was too much work to do while daylight lasted), we would at least eat a piece of sweet, fresh fruit after the meal. At other times, dessert was just as important as the rest of the meal. It was the end of the meal, and meals were the time when we gathered as a family and discussed the daily business of living.

I don't recall my mother teaching me to make desserts. I just learned how by watching her. We children always found our way to the kitchen after school or when chores were done, and as we were not distracted by television, stereo headphones, or the telephone, we absorbed a lot of what Mother was doing to prepare the meal. Later, when I moved away to live in New York, I found myself making the same desserts, almost by instinct.

Old-fashioned desserts are made with ingredients readily available in every farm kitchen: eggs, cream, butter, and sugar. They smell and taste comfortable and warm, as only a smooth custard or pudding can; or the way a blackberry roly-poly does as you taste the goodness of sweet fruit against soft, tender boiled (not baked) dough, so similar to dumpling dough. Fresh fruit cobblers, pies, and bettys are made in the summer and fall when the fruit is in season; pies and tarts with berry or fruit preserves are made in the winter to bring back the taste of summer. During the holidays fancier fruitcakes and cookies find their way to the sideboard, but even then, nothing is too precious or elaborate.

I remember how excited we were when the first peaches were ripe because we knew peach cobbler would soon be on the table. We felt the same way when we spied blackberries along the hedgerows, looking forward to the pie Mother would bake. In the summer, making ice cream with rich fresh cream and sweet, juicy berries on a hot August afternoon was a treat we could only dream about during cold, windy February. When February actually arrived, my father would gather a big pot of snow off a roof or some other unsullied place, mix it with heavy cream and vanilla, and we would eat "snow cream"—an exciting diversion during long, housebound winter days.

Sometimes my mother baked cakes in the fireplace. She put the whole cake inside a big iron pot that sat on the edge of the hearth. The lid of the pot had a rim large enough to hold pieces of coal from the fireplace and so with the fire surrounding the pot and the hot coals on top of it the cake baked quite evenly. Mother was able to tell when the cake was done by some extra sense: she just *knew*.

While I do not bake cakes or pies in a fireplace, I still carry on the custom of having something sweet in the house for drop-in guests. I remember that we children were always glad to see someone stop by, since it meant we could eat any leftovers after the guest had gone home. I now make a number of cakes, pies, and other desserts that were not part of my childhood—perhaps chocolate soufflé is the most notable—but if desserts had not been such an important part of our meals, both in everyday life and to celebrate special occasions and holidays, I probably would not bake nearly as much, or get as much pleasure from it.

Christmas was a time for lots of baking. We began to anticipate it as early as September when we gathered black walnuts, hickory nuts, and hazelnuts that later were used for cakes and cookies. I have always loved Christmas, in large part because of the wonderful sweets of the season. I set aside at least one whole day now to bake Christmas cookies. I do all the shopping at one time and then mix the doughs that taste best if they have a day or two to mellow. I plan to spend a full day in the kitchen baking. I don't answer the telephone or stop to talk with anyone. I just bake, undisturbed. There is no question about it, baking and decorating Christmas cookies is tedious, but all at once, you realize you have jars filled to the brim with pretty cookies and have spent a satisfying day in a warm, sweet-smelling kitchen. Wrapping the cookies to give to your friends is the fun part, and as I get them wrapped and labeled, I become more and more excited. Delivering them is a very important part of Christmas for me—it is a very good feeling to share with your friends something you have made.

The more you bake, the better you get at it, whether it is making cookies or cakes or pie crusts. I never stop learning, which is one reason, for example, I have several different recipes in this chapter for pie crust. Every time I make it, I discover something else, some new trick or way to combine the ingredients to make a crust that tastes just right with a particular filling.

If the crust is good, everyone will comment on it (and even if it isn't but the filling is, people still comment on the crust). One of the nicest things about pie crust is that you can always patch it if it tears—the filling will hide any imperfections.

When making dessert, use the tastiest, freshest ingredients you can find. Never cut corners here or, for that matter, in any other part of the meal. Real butter, ripe fruit, good chocolate, and fresh cream all produce the best results, and remember that a little taste of the best is far more satisfactory than a lot of a mediocre sweet.

SUMMER PUDDING

I suppose this dessert is called summer pudding because it is not cooked and because it uses whatever berries are in season at any time during the summer. Its flavor is crisp and cool, tart and refreshing. You should use sturdy white bread that is a day or so old but not too firm or stale. The pudding must set in the refrigerator overnight, so this is a good dessert to make when you need to plan ahead. If you want to, you can use all raspberries or all blackberries rather than a combination of currants and raspberries. When I made this for the James Beard Tribute Dinner in New York one year, Mayor Koch had five helpings.

SERVES 6 TO 8

2 quarts fresh-picked currants
2 pints raspberries
1½ cups granulated sugar
12 slices firm, but not too heavy,
    day-old white bread, left out
    to dry
4 to 6 tablespoons unsalted butter

½ pint heavy cream (not ultra-
    pasteurized)

2-quart bowl or nonmetallic mold
    6 inches deep and 6 inches wide at
    the top

Wash the currants, drain them, then pick off the stems. Put 2 cups of the picked currants in a nonmetallic 5-quart pot. Crush the fruit to extract the juice, then add the remaining currants. Place the pot over medium heat and simmer for 15 to 18 minutes. Remove from the burner and add 1 pint of the raspberries. When cool, pour the contents of the pot into a sieve and press the berries to remove their seeds and skins. Add sugar to the berry purée and mix well again. Taste and add more sugar, if desired.

Cut the crusts off the slices of bread and discard them. Butter the bread lightly on one side. Line the bowl with the bread, the unbuttered side against the bowl, placing a slice on the bottom of the bowl, then some slices around the sides, cutting when needed, to have the bread fit neatly in the bowl. Pour a cup of the currant and raspberry mixture into the bowl and cover with a slice of bread. Continue alternating purée and bread until the bowl is full. See

(recipe continues)

to it that the bread is well soaked with the berry mixture. Place a plate on the mixture—the plate should fit just inside of the bowl. Then fill a clean quart jar to weigh 2 pounds and place it on top of the plate. The weight of the jar will press the juices into the bread and the plate will catch any juice that is pressed out.

Set in the refrigerator overnight. Reserve any extra berry purée. Unmold the pudding onto a platter, and spoon over the reserved purée. Serve with lightly whipped cream.

Old-fashioned Custard-based Vanilla Ice Cream

I use both vanilla and a vanilla bean when I make ice cream. I can't get enough strength from a bean alone but I like to use one because beans have such good flavor. I prefer beans from Madagascar, which have a very subtle flavor, rather than Tahitian vanilla beans. And I always put a little salt in the ice cream—it really brings out the flavor. I add a pinch or two more if the flavor is not to the point I like when I am just about to freeze the ice cream. I like to make ice cream in an old-fashioned ice cream freezer with a metal dasher. The new ones have plastic dashers, which do not stay cold, and the most important thing when you are making ice cream is to have all the equipment very, very cold. This recipe is for 3 quarts of ice cream, but if you want to make less, halve the recipe. Divide the measurements for all the ingredients in half, except for the vanilla bean and the vanilla, which should stay as ½ vanilla bean and 1 table-spoon of vanilla. The amounts of ice and salt will probably remain the same, too—but they will vary anyhow, depending on the type of ice cream freezer you use. This ice cream and the sherbets that follow can all be reduced to fit any of the easy-to-use small ice cream machines available today.

MAKES 3 QUARTS

2 cups milk
½ vanilla bean, split open
4 egg yolks, lightly beaten
1 cup sugar
1 teaspoon salt
¼ cup vanilla

1 quart heavy cream

10 pounds ice
1⅓ cups table salt
Ice cream maker (3-quart capacity)

Pour the milk into a saucepan with the vanilla bean and heat over a medium-high burner until it is scalded (tiny beads will form around the edge); never allow it to boil. Have at hand a bowl containing the lightly beaten egg yolks and mix in the sugar and salt. Remove the vanilla bean and pour the milk slowly into the yolk mixture, stirring constantly.

Pour the yolk and milk mixture into a clean saucepan and set it over a

(recipe continues)

medium-high burner, stirring continuously until the milk begins to heat up. Lift the pan and hold it above the burner, then raise the heat a bit and stir with the pan still held above the heat, until a spoon dipped into the mixture is definitely coated with custard—about 3 to 4 minutes. At this point set the pan into a bowl of cold water to halt further cooking. Take the pan from the water right away and strain the custard into a bowl. When cold, add the vanilla and heavy cream. Stir well, cover, and put in the refrigerator to chill thoroughly.

It is a good idea to scald the freezer can and dasher and put them in the refrigerator to chill. Crush the ice small enough to fit properly between the freezer can and bucket. Have the crank and the salt at hand. Stir the custard well. Put the dasher in place and pour in the custard, filling the cannister three-quarters full. Attach the crank, see that it is properly locked, and turn very gently to see if it is on correctly. Plug in the freezer before filling with ice and salt. Otherwise the ice will freeze up and prevent the crank from turning. Fill with ice and salt, using three parts ice and one part salt—first a layer of ice, then salt—until the bucket is filled. Be careful not to let any salt get into the cream from the top of the can. Turn the can gently for the first few turns. Then turn as fast as you can, exchanging with someone else as you tire. The ice will be melting continuously as you turn, which is necessary to freeze the cream. Never let the ice reach the top of the can because it might get into the cream. Refill with ice and salt. As the cream begins to freeze, it will become harder to turn. Continue to turn until it becomes impossible—it takes about 25 to 30 minutes.

Unlock the crank and lift it off. Wipe off the top of the cream can as well as the sides to prevent any salt from falling in when you remove the cover. Have someone hold the cream can in place while you lift out the dasher. With a long-handled spoon, scrape the cream from the dasher. Lay the dasher on a dish or hand it to the children who are usually waiting to lick it. Dip the spoon into the cream and bring up the frozen part from the bottom by folding the top in. Do this folding motion three or four times. Smooth over and replace the cover. Pack it again with salt and ice just as you did before freezing. Cover with a burlap bag or heavy canvas. Store in a cool place or in the refrigerator for at least 2 to 3 hours before using, or put in the freezer. If you prefer, you may make the ice cream in an electric freezer following the manufacturer's instructions.

Tangerine Sherbet

After a great holiday meal, try this delightful tangerine sherbet. Tangerines have a rather short season and I like to extend it as much as possible by making sherbet. I prefer to buy tangerines from a health-food store since the rind is not sprayed. This goes for oranges and lemons also.

MAKES ABOUT 1½ QUARTS

1¼ cups sugar

1½ cups water

Grated rind of 2 tangerines

¼ teaspoon salt

5 cups strained tangerine juice (from about 20 tangerines)

Put the sugar and water in a stainless steel saucepan and cook for 10 minutes, until the sugar dissolves. Take from the heat and add the grated rind and salt. Let the mixture stand until cold and then add the tangerine juice. Stir and pour into the cannister of an ice cream maker. Freeze according to the manufacturer's instructions, as you would ice cream.

Fresh Peach Cobbler

With the first juicy, sweet peaches of summer, we always made cobbler. In Virginia, it is traditional to weave a lattice top pastry over the fruit, which is piled generously into a deep pie plate and mounded a little in the center. When you make cobbler, all you really want to taste are sweet, fresh peaches—nothing else—so use the sweetest fruit you can find. I like Nutmeg Sauce with cobbler, but at home we would just spoon the juice from the peaches up over the cobbler, which is good, too.

SERVES 4 TO 6

Butter Pie Pastry (see page 256)   ¾ cup (1½ sticks) butter
1 cup sugar   Nutmeg Sauce (see page 251)
7 large peaches

Roll out half the pie dough and press into an 8-inch pie dish that is 2 inches deep. Sprinkle with 2 tablespoons of sugar and refrigerate. Roll out the rest of the pie dough and cut into 8 strips for a lattice top. Lay the strips between wax paper and refrigerate. The dough will keep in the refrigerator for several hours.

About 1½ hours before you plan to bake the cobbler, take the pie dough and the strips from the refrigerator.

Preheat the oven to 450°F.

Peel and slice the peaches. Sprinkle half of the remaining sugar over the pie crust and lay the sliced peaches in the pie plate. Mound the last few slices in the center. Sprinkle the rest of the sugar over the fruit and dot with thin slices of butter. Weave the pastry strips over the fruit, four going one way and four the other. Moisten the rim of the pie with cold water and press the strips down to seal.

Set the cobbler on the middle rack of the oven and bake for 10 minutes. Lower the heat to 425°F, and bake for another 35 minutes. Let the cobbler cool for about 30 minutes before serving with Nutmeg Sauce.

NUTMEG SAUCE

While I like this sauce with a number of desserts, I always serve it with Plum Pudding and Fresh Peach Cobbler. I use dried orange peel to flavor the sauce, which I make by drying orange peel on a rack for several days at room temperature. Scrape the white pith from the peel before drying it. The dried peel, which has good orange flavor, keeps for weeks in a covered jar and you can use it as you need it.

MAKES ABOUT 1½ CUPS

⅔ cup sugar

Pinch salt

2 teaspoons cornstarch

¼ teaspoon freshly grated nutmeg

1 cup boiling water

2-inch piece dried orange peel

3 tablespoons brandy

Mix the sugar, salt, cornstarch, and nutmeg together in a small saucepan. Pour the boiling water into the pan and stir. Add the orange peel and gently boil over medium heat for 12 minutes. If you cook it much longer, the flavor will not be as good. Take the saucepan from the burner and stir in the brandy. Cover the pan and set aside until needed. When you are ready to serve the sauce, reheat it over low heat. Do let it come to a boil. Lift out the orange peel before serving.

Freezing Blackberries, Blueberries, Raspberries, Gooseberries, and Currants

The season for berries is so short, I freeze as many as I am able to so that I can get the fresh taste in pies and tarts all year long. I use blueberries to make a sweet sauce for pancakes and gooseberries for a sauce for meat and game.

Neither raspberries nor currants should be washed before they are frozen because they become soggy. Rinse other kinds of berries in a colander and then spread them out on towels to dry thoroughly. When they are dry, lay them on cookie sheets in single layers and freeze them for about 20 minutes. After 20 minutes, they are firm enough to be put into clean, dry milk cartons or freezer-safe Mason jars for long-term freezing. Because they are already frozen they will not stick together in the jars but will be like marbles. Tape the cartons shut or screw the Mason jar lids on tight. When you want some berries, you need only to take as many as you will use.

PIE PLATES

When I make fruit pies I like to use Pyrex pie plates. The crust browns better in them. Also, acidic fruit can react to a tin pie plate and taste a little metallic.

Raspberry Pie Garnished with Whipped Cream

For this pie, you need 3 pints of raspberries, because raspberries cook down so much. The juice from the berries is used as a glaze and the whole thing is pretty and sweet and really delicious, especially when served with whipped cream. I specify organic raspberries simply because I think they taste better.

When I make the buttery crust that I think tastes best with light-tasting fruits and berries, I do something that might be too fussy for most cooks. You don't have to do it, but it makes a nice crust. I chop up the butter, put it in the freezer, and let it get really frozen. I then take 1 cup of flour and cut in the frozen butter, mixing it in well—you have to work really fast before the butter softens too much. When this mixture is fine enough, similar to cornmeal, I add the rest of the flour and proceed with the recipe. The crust is nice and light and good with berry and lemon meringue pies.

BUTTER PIE PASTRY

2 cups unbleached all-purpose flour

Scant teaspoon salt

12 tablespoons (1½ sticks) firmly chilled or frozen butter, cut into small pieces

¼ cup ice water

PIE FILLING

3 pints raspberries, organic if possible

½ cup sugar

About 1 cup sweetened whipped cream

9-inch pie plate

To make the pie pastry: Put the flour, salt, and butter in a mixing bowl. Blend well with a pastry blender or the tips of your fingers, until the mixture is the texture of cornmeal. Add the ice water, mix quickly, and shape the dough into a ball. Dust the dough lightly with flour and shape into a flat cake. Wrap in wax paper and put in the refrigerator to rest for 30 minutes.

Preheat the oven to 425°F.

Remove the dough from the refrigerator and divide it into 2 unequal pieces. Roll the larger piece out and press it into a 9-inch pie dish; trim the edges. Roll out the second piece of dough into a 7-inch circle and trim the edges in a zigzag design. Stamp out a 2-inch circle from the center of the top crust, using a round cookie cutter. Put the top crust in a pie plate and bake for 12 to 15 minutes. Lift the crust from the pie plate and cool on a wire rack.

Before baking the bottom shell, prick the surface without piercing all the way through to the pie plate. This will prevent the pastry from puffing up. Check the pastry after 10 minutes of baking. Prick any puffed-up places and continue to cook until lightly browned. Cool before filling.

To make the filling: Pick the raspberries over, looking for any moldy ones or stems. Do not wash the berries or they will become soggy. Put the berries in a wide ovenproof dish in a single layer. Sprinkle 3 tablespoons of the sugar over them and set them in a preheated 375°F oven for 12 to 13 minutes. This should be time enough for the berries to bleed and give out the right amount of juice.

Remove the berries from the oven and cool. Then lift each berry onto another dish and scrape the juice from the ovenproof dish into a stainless steel saucepan. Add the remaining sugar and set the pan over a medium burner. Cook for 12 to 13 minutes, until the juice is reduced to a thick syrup. Remove this from the stove and hold until you are ready to assemble the pie.

Brush the bottom of the cooled pie shell with some of the heavy syrup. Line the shell with a single layer of raspberries. Reserve 8 or 9 berries. Pile up the rest of the raspberries in the shell to make a thick pie. Spoon the syrup glaze over the berries, making sure to coat all of them. Position the pastry top over the berries. Fill in the stamped-out center with the reserved berries and spoon glaze over them. Serve sweetened whipped cream on the side.

NOTE:

If you are making the pie pastry for another pie, there is no need to stamp out the center of the top crust. This is simply for decorative purposes for the raspberry pie.

Pastry Shells

3 cups unbleached all-purpose flour

Scant teaspoon salt

1 cup (2 sticks) firmly chilled or frozen butter, cut into small pieces

¼ cup or more ice water

Put the flour, salt, and butter in a mixing bowl. Blend well with a pastry blender or the tips of your fingers, until the mixture is the texture of cornmeal. Add ¼ cup ice water, mix quickly, and shape the dough into a ball. If it is too dry to shape, add a few more drops ice water. Dust the dough lightly with flour and shape into a flat cake. Wrap in wax paper and put in the refrigerator to rest for at least 30 minutes.

Preheat the oven to 425°F.

When you are ready to bake the shells, divide the dough into 4 equal pieces. Roll out each piece of dough on a lightly floured surface until very thin and about 5½ inches round or square, depending on the shape of the tart pans. Roll 1 piece of dough around the rolling pin and gently unroll it over a small tartlet tin or ovenproof 4-ounce ramekin. Trim the edges and press the dough into the form.

Prick each shell all over with a fork to prevent puffing during baking. Check after 4 minutes and deflate any puffy spots with a fork. Be careful not to pierce all the way through the pastry. Bake the shells until nicely browned, 10 to 12 minutes altogether. Remove them from the oven, cool, and fill with the filling of your choice.

LARD PIE PASTRY

I developed this particular pie pastry for mincemeat filling but it is good with juicy fillings such as berries and apples. Lard (see box on page 260) gives a crispy crust, richer than butter. Sometimes I think it is flakier than butter, too. I grew up with lard pastry and I guess I like its flavor. Making any pastry is tricky and for this one, the lard has to be really cold. I put it in the freezer for at least 20 minutes, or for as long as overnight, before I make the pastry. When I bake this or any other crust without filling, I don't use pie weights or foil. I think they make the pastry heavy. I prick the dough lightly all over—not all the way through—and then bake it. After about 10 minutes, I take it from the oven and prick it anywhere it needs to deflate. If you don't prick it, it will blister. But even if it does, when it is filled, it will flatten out.

MAKES 2 DOUBLE-CRUST OR 3 SINGLE-CRUST PIES

3 cups unbleached all-purpose flour	¾ cup (6 ounces) chilled lard, cut into
1 teaspoon salt	pieces
	½ cup plus 2 tablespoons ice water

Place the flour, salt, and chilled lard in a mixing bowl and blend with a pastry blender or your fingertips until it is the texture of cornmeal, blending quickly to prevent warming the lard. Sprinkle the ice water over the dough. Quickly mix with a stout wooden spoon. Pull the dough together into a ball and turn it onto a lightly floured surface. Dust the ball lightly with flour, then divide the dough into 2 or 3 equal pieces (depending on whether you want 2 double-crust or 3 single-crust pies). Shape into cakes and wrap each in wax paper. Place in the refrigerator for 30 minutes or overnight.

For single-crust pies, roll the 3 pieces out thin and place each in an 8- or 9-inch pie plate (the size depends on the depth of the plate). The pastry-lined pans can be wrapped in wax paper and kept in the refrigerator or freezer until needed. If you want double-crust pies, roll out the 2 pastry pieces and then put the trimmings together to make the bottom crusts. Letting the pie pastry rest overnight definitely produces a more perfectly baked pie—that is, the crust comes out with a good shape.

Lard

Although you can buy lard in supermarkets (usually in the refrigerated section where butter and margarine are displayed), I suggest buying it from a butcher. He should be able to get some that has not been hydrogenated, a process that I think makes lard waxy and difficult to dissolve. The best is made from what is called leaf lard, which is a sheet of fat pulled from the vent area of the pig—your butcher should know what you mean when you ask for it. You might also be able to get leaf lard in the supermarket—ask the butcher.

Blackberry or Boysenberry Pie

These days, I like boysenberries almost better than blackberries because they are so sweet and delicious. Longer and fleshier than blackberries, boysenberries are not quite as black. Blackberries, which grow along fields and in swampy places and hedgerows, are more compact and taste tarter than cultivated boysenberries.

MAKES ONE 9-INCH PIE

Lard Pie Pastry (see page 259) for one 9-inch double crust

4 cups fresh or frozen and defrosted blackberries or boysenberries

⅓ cup sugar

Rounded ¼ teaspoon freshly grated nutmeg

1 tablespoon cornstarch

3 or 4 thin slices chilled butter

It is good to have a pastry-lined pie plate ready at hand before preparing the berries. Pastry can be made days ahead, put into a pie plate, well covered, and set in the refrigerator or freezer. If the berries are fresh, pick them over, removing any spoiled ones or any stems. Wash and drain the berries.

Mix together the sugar, nutmeg, and cornstarch. Toss the berries into the pie pastry and see that they are evenly spread out. Sprinkle the sugar mixture evenly over the berries. Break up the thin slices of butter and distribute them over the sugar mixture.

Roll the top pie crust onto a rolling pin. Pick up the rolling pin and unroll the crust over the pie plate. Trim off the edges, making the top crust even with the edges of the pie plate. Lift the top edge and wet the rim, then press down all around with a fork. Make about 6 decorative 1-inch slashes over the top of the pie. This is important to release steam and give a crisper crust to the pie.

Set the pie in a preheated 425°F oven for 45 minutes—juicy pies need this high heat to ensure that the crust is crisp. However, you can reduce the heat to 375°F after 25 minutes if the pie is browning too quickly; check after 35 minutes. When the juice comes through the top crust, the pie is about done. You should not overcook the pie. After you have removed it from the oven, it will continue to cook until it cools off. It is better if you can bake your pies as late as possible before serving them. They are at their best served slightly warm from the oven with a crispy crust and juicy insides.

RED CURRANT PIE

When I make this pie, I use only red currants because when you cook the white ones they dissolve into oblivion. Even with the red currants you need 6 cups; they collapse when they are cooked. I grew up with both white and red currants and nearly everyone had them in the garden, but today they are a little difficult to find. When I see them I buy a lot and freeze some (see page 252). They keep their color and flavor so well when they are frozen, it hardly matters whether you use fresh or frozen for the pie. I buy them most often at New York's Union Square Greenmarket when they are in season in early July. Even though there seems to be a whole generation that grew up never tasting currants, there is interest in them. Sometimes people ask me: "What are you going to do with those berries?" And once, after tasting a currant, a woman shopping at the Greenmarket said, "Why, it's not even sweet!"

MAKES ONE 9-INCH PIE

Lard Pie Pastry (see page 259) for one
   9-inch double crust
1 egg white
⅔ cup sugar

6 cups fresh or frozen and defrosted
   currants
¼ cup cornstarch
4 thin slices chilled butter
Whipped cream (optional)

Preheat the oven to 425°F.

Have your 9-inch pie plate lined with the pastry. Paint the bottom of the pastry with the egg white and sprinkle 1 tablespoon of sugar over it. Leave pastry out to dry for 30 minutes before filling. Fill the pie plate with the currants. Mix together the remaining sugar and the cornstarch, and pour this over the currants. Dot with 4 thin slices of butter. Then cover the pie with the top pastry shell. Lift the pastry up along the edges and moisten the bottom rim. Seal down the top edges by pressing a table fork all around. This gives a nice decoration and seals the pie at the same time. Trim the edges and pierce 6 slashes in the top of the pastry to let the steam out during baking. Put the pie in the oven and bake for 45 minutes. (A very juicy pie requires a hot oven to brown properly; see remarks in preceding recipe about baking at this heat.) Remove from the oven and serve warm, with whipped cream if you like.

WILD PERSIMMON TARTS

The flavor of wild persimmons is so sweet and delicate you need a thin, crisp crust such as the one here to set them off. The crust serves the same purpose as a cone for ice cream—you almost don't *need* to eat it, but it tastes good. Wild persimmons are about the size of a quarter and have big seeds. You really have to buy a couple of quarts to be sure you can get at least 1½ pints of pulp. You can use cultivated persimmons; however, the flavor will be different—but still good. I make these little tarts in a muffin pan, individual tart pans, or any other 3-inch forms. To make them extra pretty, I put spun sugar tops on each tart. When you spin sugar, you can easily pick it up and shape it to fit over the tarts. Don't worry if the shape isn't perfectly round.

SERVES 5

2 quarts wild or cultivated persimmons

TART DOUGH

1 cup unbleached all-purpose flour

Pinch salt

¼ teaspoon almond extract

¼ cup sugar

6 tablespoons (¾ stick) unsalted
 butter

1 egg yolk

Whipped cream made with ½ cup
 heavy cream, 2 teaspoons sugar,
 and 2 teaspoons raspberry liqueur

5 spun sugar tops (see page 299)

Rinse the persimmons under cold tap water. Drain dry. Remove the caps and take out the seeds. Press the pulp through a sieve into a bowl. Cover and set in the refrigerator until needed.

Put the flour, salt, almond extract, sugar, and butter in a mixing bowl. Stir the egg yolk and add it to the flour mixture. Blend well with your fingertips until the dough becomes smooth and pliable. Shape into a circle. Wrap lightly in wax paper and put in the refrigerator for 15 to 20 minutes, until firm. Remove from the refrigerator and roll out on a lightly dusted surface, dusting the rolling pin with flour. Roll the dough very thin; it is intended just to hold the persimmon pulp.

Preheat the oven to 400°F.

(recipe continues)

Cut out the tart pastries to fill five 3-inch shells. Press the pastry into each tart pan, crimp the edges with a fork, and prick the surface of the pastry well to keep the crust from puffing up. Bake for 7 to 10 minutes, until light brown and crisp. Remove from the oven, cool, and store in a tin lined with wax paper until ready to use.

Fill the shells with the chilled persimmon pulp and garnish with a thin ribbon of sweetened whipped cream flavored with the raspberry liqueur. Top each tart with a spun sugar top just before serving.

TYLER PIE

When I was a child we always had this pie in the off season, when there weren't berries and fruit. It's made with the ingredients every housewife always had in the kitchen: eggs, butter, milk, and flour and is an easy pie to make. Although I was not aware of it as a young girl, the origin of the pie's name comes from the Tyler family. President Tyler, who was born in Orange County, Virginia, is said to have been very fond of it, as were the other members of his family and generations to follow. I only knew that everyone made Tyler pie. It is much like chess pie—they are both everyday Southern pies made with almost exactly the same ingredients, but still they taste a little different. In the South there's a big stir about how chess pie got its name. Some say it's because when a guest would say "My, this a good pie, what is it called?" the answer would be "jes pie." For this version of Tyler pie, I add grated fresh coconut. I think the Tylers did, too.

SERVES 6 OR 7

Lard Pie Pastry (see page 259) for one
   8-inch pie shell
2 eggs
¾ cup sugar
1 teaspoon flour
½ teaspoon salt

½ cup (1 stick) unsalted butter, melted
   but not quite liquid
1 teaspoon vanilla
1 teaspoon lemon extract
1 cup milk, at room temperature
½ cup freshly grated coconut (see
   page 288)

Line an 8-inch pie plate with the pastry. Do not bake the pastry. Chill until ready to cook.

Preheat the oven to 350°F.

Beat the eggs well, then add the sugar mixed with flour and salt. Mix well and add the butter, vanilla, and lemon extract. Stir thoroughly and pour in the milk. Mix well and then add the grated coconut. Pour the mixture into the pastry-lined pan, seeing to it that the coconut is evenly spread throughout the custard. Bake in the preheated oven for 30 to 35 minutes, until set and golden brown.

DAMSON PLUM PIE

This, too, is a real old Southern recipe that probably originally came from England, since damson plum pies were made during Colonial times. Damson plums are Old World plums that are very small and very sour. They have been cultivated so that now the younger trees produce larger-sized plums, but we have an old tree in our yard that has little plums. Large or small, they are in season in August and only a few grocers carry them. You can buy damson plum preserves or make your own for this recipe, but if you use other plum preserves, the pie will not have the same sharp flavor.

SERVES 8

CRUST

1 cup unbleached all-purpose flour

¼ teaspoon salt

5 tablespoons chilled lard

1½ to 2 tablespoons ice water

FILLING

3 eggs

¾ cup light brown sugar

1 teaspoon flour

⅛ teaspoon salt

3 tablespoons melted unsalted butter

1 teaspoon vanilla

¾ cup Damson Plum Preserves, with pits removed (see page 186)

Whipped cream, for garnish

For the crust, mix the flour, salt, and lard in a large mixing bowl, using a pastry blender or your fingertips. Blend until the mixture resembles fine crumbs. Add half of the ice water, then mix the dough by hand. Pull the moist dough together gently and add small amounts of water until the dough holds together. Shape the dough into a ball, and refrigerate for 20 minutes. Roll out the dough on a lightly floured surface. Press the dough into a 9-inch pie or tart pan, fluting the edges. Cover and refrigerate or freeze until ready to use, at least 30 minutes.

Preheat the oven to 350°F.

For the filling, beat the eggs in a mixing bowl until light. Mix in the sugar, flour, and salt. Add the butter and vanilla, mixing well. Stir in the preserves. Pour into the prepared pie shell, making sure the pieces of plum are well distributed. Bake until set, about 45 minutes. Serve at room temperature. Garnish with a ribbon of whipped cream.

MINCEMEAT TARTS WITH BRANDY BUTTER

Mincemeat pie is as much a part of Christmas as oysters and plum pudding. The filling tastes better after it ages awhile and, with proper storage, can last for as long as five years (not that I have been able to keep it nearly that long). For its full flavor to come out, you must store it for at least three weeks, so plan your holiday baking to give yourself plenty of time. If you store it for a month or more, add extra rum or wine to the mincemeat.

As much as I like mincemeat pie, lately I have preferred these individual tarts, which can be made a few days ahead of time. The idea for adding rum butter to the tarts was given to me by an English lady who so liked the mincemeat in *The Taste of Country Cooking* she kindly wrote to me saying mine was the first recipe she had seen in a long time that actually used meat. This is the same recipe with very minor alterations. One day she sent me these little tarts flavored with rum butter and I just loved them. The rum butter, spooned under the pastry lids just after they are baked or at the time of reheating, blends deliciously with the mincemeat filling as it melts.

MAKES ENOUGH FOR 8 TARTS

FILLING

½ pound bottom round beef	½ teaspoon ground cloves
2 ounces suet (from veal kidney is best)	½ teaspoon ground ginger
2 ounces currants	½ nutmeg, freshly grated
1 ounce seedless raisins	½ teaspoon salt
1½ ounces muscat raisins, seeds removed	½ cup Madeira
	½ cup rum
1 ounce candied orange peel	½ cup brandy
1 ounce candied lemon peel	½ cup apple cider
1½ cups chopped tart apples	
⅓ cup (packed) dark brown sugar	1½-gallon stone or glass crock, sterilized
½ teaspoon ground cinnamon	
½ teaspoon ground allspice	Lard Pie Pastry (see page 259)

BRANDY BUTTER

1 cup (2 sticks) unsalted butter	1 tablespoon brandy
1 cup confectioners' sugar	

Put the beef in a saucepan with enough water to cover. Simmer the meat for 1 hour, then take it from the heat. Let it cool in the liquid, and when it is completely cool, lift it from the pan and chop into very small pieces. Remove the skin from the suet and chop the fat by hand until it is almost as smooth as lard.

Put the fruit in a bowl and stir with a clean wooden spoon. Sprinkle the brown sugar, spices, salt, and suet over the fruit and stir well. Add the beef and broth to the fruit. Mix the Madeira, rum, brandy, and cider together, and pour over the fruit and beef, stirring well. Spoon the mincemeat into the sterilized crock and cover the crock with a clean white cloth. Tie the cloth around the mouth of the crock with a piece of twine and set a plate on top of it. Put the crock in a cool, dark, dry spot and let it age for at least 3 weeks before using it in mincemeat pie or tarts.

Preheat the oven to 375°F.

To make the tarts: Roll out the dough. Rub the inside of an 8-cup muffin tin with unsalted butter. Cut the tart dough to fit the bottom and sides of each cup of the muffin tin. At the same time, cut out pastry disks that will fit over the tops of the tarts, using scraps of pastry. Press the pastry into the buttered muffin cups, and spoon enough mincemeat filling into each one to fill the tarts to the rims. Set the pastry tops over the mincemeat. Do not crimp the pastry as you will be lifting the tops off the baked tarts when you add the brandy butter.

Bake the tarts for 20 minutes, until the pastry tops are lightly browned.

(recipe continues)

Lower the heat to 325°F, and bake for 15 minutes more. Watch the tarts carefully to make sure they do not dry out or get too browned.

If you are planning to serve the tarts right away, make the brandy butter while they are baking. Cream the butter until light, then gradually add the sugar until well mixed. Stir in the brandy. When the tarts are done turn them out onto a wire rack. While still hot, using the handle of a teaspoon, gently lift the pastry lids off the tarts and spoon a teaspoon of brandy butter into each tart, directly on the filling. Replace the lids and serve the tarts warm with extra brandy butter on the side, if you like.

If you have made the tarts ahead and plan to serve them in 3 or 4 days, do not prepare and add in the brandy butter now but let the tarts cool. When cool, store them in a covered tin.

To reheat the tarts, preheat the oven to 325°F. Lift off the lids now and spoon the brandy butter inside, then set the tarts on a baking sheet and bake for 12 to 13 minutes, or until heated through.

Marinated Apple Tart with Custard Sauce

I use Staymen Winesap apples when I marinate apples this way—the flesh is crisp and the flavor is "winey" without being too tart and blends well with the liquors. Staymen Winesaps are the oldest variety of Winesap apples; if you cannot find them, try Granny Smith apples. Both are delicious marinated and you will find that their flavor is nicely heightened by the syrup. I got the idea for marinating apples once when I was chopping some to add to mincemeat. "If this keeps," I thought, "the apples alone should keep, too." And they do—for a couple of months, although they probably would keep for a couple of years if you could manage to hang on to them for that long before eating them. After they have marinated for a month or two, I like to make them into a tart, such as this one, but you can also cook marinated apples in a casserole with a mixture of other fresh fruits and berries and serve it with custard sauce.

Usually I make the tart at Christmastime. I marinate the apples in the early fall when they are plentiful and fresh in the markets and by December they are perfect for the tart.

The custard sauce is lightly flavored with almond extract, which could be left out if you want a vanilla custard. You could also increase the amount of almond extract to 1 teaspoon and reduce the measure of vanilla to ¼ teaspoon for more almond flavor. Do not leave out the vanilla bean. It gives the custard smooth, deep flavor. I love custard sauce and spoon it over just about anything sweet. If I have fresh fruit or berries, I make vanilla ice cream, scatter the fruit over the ice cream, and serve it with custard sauce. I ladle it over pies, such as this one, and like to eat it plain right off the spoon. The trick to making a good custard is to use a fork to break the egg yolks rather than a whisk—that beats too much air into the yolks. Next, slowly stir the scalded milk (brought just to the boil) into the yolks with a stainless steel or wooden spoon. When you return the mixture to the saucepan, stir it constantly *over low heat,* being sure to scrape around the sides of the pan all the while.

MAKES ONE 8-INCH TART AND 2½ CUPS CUSTARD SAUCE

MARINATED APPLES

3 pounds apples, preferably Staymen Winesap	¼ cup sugar
	¼ cup rum

(recipe continues)

¼ cup brandy	1 egg white, lightly beaten
½ cup Madeira	7 tablespoons sugar
	1 tablespoon butter

½ recipe Lard Pie Pastry (see page 259)

CUSTARD SAUCE

2 cups milk	¼ teaspoon salt
½ vanilla bean, split lengthwise	1 teaspoon vanilla
4 egg yolks	¼ teaspoon almond extract
⅓ cup sugar	

To marinate the apples: Peel the apples and then cut them into quarters. Core them and cut each quarter into 4 even slices so that you have 16 slices from each apple. Layer the apple slices in a crock and sprinkle them with the sugar. Pour the rum, brandy, and Madeira over the apples. Cover with a cloth or lid, and let the the crock stand in a cool, dry place for 2 to 3 months or longer.

To make the tart: When you are ready to make the tart, preheat the oven to 375°F.

Roll out the pie pastry to fit an 8-inch tart pan. Brush the bottom of the pastry with the egg white to prevent it from getting soggy during baking. Sprinkle the pastry with 2 tablespoons of sugar.

Drain the apples from the crock and reserve ⅓ cup of the rum syrup. Heat the butter in a wide frying pan, and when it begins to foam, add half of the drained apples. Stir the apples as they cook over medium heat, gently turning them over and over to make sure they are well buttered. Cook them for about 8 minutes without letting them break into pieces. Let them cool a little.

Carefully spoon the other half of the apples, those that are not cooked, into

the pastry-lined tart pan. Arrange them so that they are as flat as possible. Lift the sautéed apples from the pan and place them over the uncooked apples in a pretty pattern. The cooked apples keep the uncooked apples moist during baking.

Bake the tart for 40 to 45 minutes, until the apples are tender. Take the tart from the oven and set it aside before serving. It may be served slightly warm or at room temperature.

To make the custard sauce: Scald the milk in a saucepan with the split vanilla bean. Watch it carefully and when tiny beads form around the edges of the milk, remove the pan from the burner.

Using a fork, lightly beat the egg yolks with the sugar and salt. Slowly add the scalded milk to the bowl, stirring constantly with a stainless steel or wooden spoon. Return the custard to the saucepan and cook over low heat, stirring around the sides of the pan until the custard is thick enough to coat the spoon. This will take 7 to 10 minutes. When the spoon is heavily coated with custard sauce, take the pan from the burner and set it in a bowl of ice water to stop the cooking and prevent curdling. Strain the custard into a bowl and when cool, stir in the vanilla and almond extracts. Store the custard in a covered glass jar in the refrigerator until needed.

Put the reserved syrup and the remaining 5 tablespoons of sugar in a small saucepan and reduce over medium heat until thick, about 15 minutes. Just before serving, spoon the reduced syrup over the tart as a glaze. Serve the tart with the custard sauce passed on the side.

POACHED PEARS

Fall pears taste stronger than any other pears and, in my opinion, none are as good as fall Bartletts. Bartletts reappear in the markets in the spring but never taste quite the same as the local autumn ones. Sweet and full of flavor, they perfume the kitchen as they poach, and, when they are done, come out pretty and white—unlike other pears, which sometimes lose color.

SERVES 10

4 cups sugar
3 quarts water
1 vanilla bean

10 pears
Rich Custard (see page 297)

Put the sugar, water, and the vanilla bean, split into two pieces but not separated, in a deep 4-quart stainless steel or enamel pot. Bring to a boil over high heat. Peel the pears, leaving the stem intact. Rinse under the tap to clear off any pieces of skin. Drop the pears into the pot, cover, and repeat the process as quickly as possible, dropping each pear in after peeling it, and then covering the pot again. When the last pear has been added, cover and leave the pears to simmer briskly for 25 minutes. Remove from the stove and leave covered until they are cool. Put the cooled pears in a glass container or a deep bowl, and serve at room temperature or chilled with Rich Custard. To preserve the color, it is important to keep the pears covered during cooking and afterward; otherwise they will turn dark.

Apple Brown Betty

This is one of my long-time favorite desserts. I have been making apple brown betty nearly every fall since I can remember and still love it for its simplicity and sweet fruit flavor. Early in the fall, when the apples are freshest, you may not need to add water to the recipe, but later, as the apples dry out a little, you will need it. I have found McIntosh apples are just about perfect for this dessert, but use any firm, slightly tart apple. If you have leftover French bread, it makes very good crumbs, but any day-old firm white bread will do. Whatever kind of bread you use, be sure to leave it out on the counter to dry for several hours before cutting it into cubes. Brown bettys should be served still warm. If they are allowed to get too cool, they will collapse a little. This is delicious with Custard Sauce (see page 272).

SERVES 4

1½ teaspoons freshly grated nutmeg	Grated rind of 1 lemon
½ cup sugar	2 pounds large apples
3 cups ¼-inch bread cubes	2 to 4 tablespoons cold water
2 tablespoons melted butter	(optional)

Preheat the oven to 375°F.

Combine the nutmeg and the sugar and set aside 2 tablespoons. Put the bread cubes in a bowl and toss with the rest of the sugar mixture, the melted butter, and the lemon rind.

Peel, core, and slice the apples into fairly thick wedges. Line the bottom of a heavy 1½-quart casserole with 1 cup of the bread cubes. Layer half the apples over the bread and top with ½ cup of the bread cubes. Layer the rest of the apples in the casserole and sprinkle with water. Cover with the rest of the bread cubes and evenly sprinkle the reserved 2 tablespoons of sugar over the top. Put the lid on the casserole or cover tightly with foil. Bake in the center of the preheated oven for 40 minutes. Take the lid off the betty, and bake for 10 to 15 minutes longer, or until the apples are tender and the topping is brown.

BAKED STAYMEN WINESAP APPLES WITH RICH CUSTARD SAUCE

I do not think of baked apples as a real dessert because they are not very sweet. But there are so many good baking apples in the markets in the fall, such as Staymen Winesaps, Ida Reds, and Granny Smiths, that I always like to bake some as a snack or quick dessert. These varieties bake up quickly without too much wrinkling.

SERVES 5

5 Staymen Winesap apples, about the
    same size
5 teaspoons sugar
½ teaspoon freshly grated nutmeg

1 tablespoon butter
1 cup cold water or apple cider
Rich Custard Sauce (see page 297)

Preheat the oven to 350°F.

Wash the apples under cold running water and drain. Core the apples from the blossom end with an apple corer, being careful not to punch through the bottom of the apple so the juice won't run out during cooking. To make the baked apple look more attractive, peel off a band, about ¼ inch wide, around the middle of each apple. Fill each apple with 1 teaspoon of sugar and a little nutmeg, and top with about ½ teaspoon of butter.

Arrange the prepared apples in a dish or casserole and surround with the cold water or apple cider. Set the casserole in the preheated oven and bake for 1½ hours, basting the apples occasionally as they cook. Remove from the oven and serve warm with Rich Custard Sauce.

CHESTNUTS WITH CHOCOLATE GLAZE

SERVES 4

1 pound chestnuts, prepared as
   described in box on
   page 278

1 tablespoon rum
1 ounce (1 square) semisweet chocolate

Blend the warm shelled chestnuts until smooth in a blender, food processor, or food mill. Add the rum and mix well. Spoon them into a serving dish. Put the chocolate square in the top of a double boiler and melt it over hot water. Dribble the melted chocolate over the chestnuts.

CHESTNUTS

When I was growing up in Virginia, chestnuts were as much a part of the fall nut harvest as hickory nuts, butternuts, and black walnuts. We eagerly looked forward to roasting them in the fireplace ashes and grown-ups ate them while sipping sherry and chatting before the fire. My grandfather had a chestnut grove, but now chestnut trees have disappeared in this country. Nowadays it seems that come September, we are flooded with chestnuts from Italy right up until Christmas, which is fortunate because Italian chestnuts are the best!

Some people shy away from chestnuts since they are so hard to clean. I have found that the easiest way to handle them is to cut the outer shell off, put them in a pot of really hot water, and then let it come to a boil. Uncover the pot and simmer the chestnuts for about 12 minutes. Remove from the burner. Lift them one at a time from the hot water and, holding them in a dish towel, peel off the brown inside skin with a sharp knife. Don't let the chestnuts dry before you peel them or you will never get the skin off. If I am not going to use them right away, I wrap the cleaned chestnuts in a foil packet and freeze them. Just let them defrost and use them for sauces, stuffings, or purées.

It is a good idea to buy chestnuts when they are first in the markets in late September and early October and freeze any you plan to use later in the year, cleaned and prepared as described above. Grocers often display them outside, but they should not become chilled; it spoils the flavor.

PRALINES

Pralines are not exactly easy to make. The sugar has to reach a certain temperature or otherwise the candy will not harden. I test for this temperature by dropping a little syrup in a glass of ice water. If it forms a soft mass between the thumb and forefinger—the soft-ball stage—it is ready. Also, these candies seem to work best on a clear, dry day. And if you keep them for a week before eating, their flavor seems to heighten. Sometimes I break up the praline and mix it into vanilla ice cream and then pour chocolate sauce over the ice cream. At the end of a rich meal, these pralines call for a cup of strong black Louisiana chicory coffee to wash them down.

MAKES ABOUT 12

2 cups packed light brown sugar
⅔ cup boiling water
1 tablespoon freshly squeezed lemon
    juice

1 teaspoon vanilla
1 cup chopped pecans

Put the sugar in a 1½-quart heavy saucepan, pour in the boiling water, mix well, and set the pan over medium heat. When the sugar dissolves, raise the heat, stirring thoroughly. Boil briskly until the soft-ball stage is reached—that is, when some of the syrup dropped into ice water forms a soft mass when gathered between your thumb and forefinger; start testing for the soft-ball stage after 5 minutes of cooking. Remove the pan from the stove and add the lemon juice and vanilla. Cool to lukewarm and mix in the chopped pecans, stirring the mixture until creamy soft but not firm. Spoon rounded cakes of the batter, about 1½ inches in diameter, onto a flat dish. See that the cakes are cold and hardened before storing them in a nonplastic container lined with wax paper.

PRALINES FOR SPRINKLING

When you are cooking sugar, you have to watch it carefully. Sugar scorches quicker than anything else and so once it starts to melt, you just have to stay at the stove and turn the temperature up or down. Sometimes I shake the pan a little but I never stir the sugar. A heavy pan helps a lot to keep the sugar from burning. For the best flavor, the syrup has to be a clear amber before the nuts are added. You really must put in a good amount of nuts so that the praline crushes easily. Store the crushed praline in a covered jar for several days. I like it sprinkled over ice cream.

MAKES ABOUT 2 CUPS

1 cup sugar   1 cup chopped pecans

Put the sugar in a heavy skillet and set over medium-high heat. When it begins to melt, watch it carefully and do not let it scorch or the pralines will taste bitter. Do not stir. Watch until all the sugar is melted, adjusting the heat up or down to prevent burning but to keep it melting. When the syrup turns a nice amber color, add the pecans. Stir and pour the mixture onto a lightly buttered dish or marble to cool and harden. When cold, take a rolling pin and crush the praline into pieces. Store them in a closed tin. It is best to use the crushed praline up at once, since it does not keep too well.

CHOCOLATE SOUFFLÉ

I never imagined when I first made chocolate soufflé at Café Nicholson that it would become one of the recipes for which I am best known. It was the late 1940s and I was trying to come up with a dessert for the Manhattan restaurant on East 58 Street that was a little different and very good, too. This dark, slightly bitter-tasting soufflé was a quick success with the customers.

A good chocolate soufflé depends a lot on the chocolate. I use Baker's, which is just right for the intense, not-too-sweet chocolate flavor. I have changed the recipe a little since those days at Café Nicholson, but the soufflé is still served with chocolate sauce and sweetened whipped cream to balance the flavors—nothing tastes too sweet or too bitter.

Soufflés are flexible and won't fall if you don't overcook them, something I found out at the café. You see, when a soufflé is finished cooking, it has nothing else to do but collapse. I learned that if I took the soufflé out of the oven when it was a little undercooked, by the time I carried it to the customer, it was perfectly done. This was most true for the customers seated at the far end of the restaurant's long garden—a fairly long walk from the kitchen. I can't give you precise timing advice—you will have to figure it out on your own—but just don't let a soufflé stay in the oven past its time.

I think soufflés look prettier served in individual 4-inch, 8-ounce ramekins. Take them from the oven a minute or two before the 12-minute cooking time is up, and let them finish cooking outside the oven.

SERVES 4

HOT CHOCOLATE SAUCE

1½ ounces (1½ squares) unsweetened chocolate, grated

1 tablespoon sugar

1½ cups cold water

1 teaspoon vanilla

SOUFFLÉ

1 cup milk

4-inch piece vanilla bean, or 1 teaspoon vanilla

4 ounces (4 squares) unsweetened chocolate, grated

3 tablespoons butter

⅓ cup hot water

(recipe continues)

2 large egg yolks

¼ teaspoon salt

3 tablespoons sugar

4 to 5 teaspoons butter, softened

1⅓ cups egg whites

3 tablespoons confectioners' sugar

VANILLA-FLAVORED SWEETENED
WHIPPED CREAM

1 cup heavy cream

3 tablespoons sugar

1 teaspoon vanilla

Four 8-ounce soufflé dishes, or one
2-quart soufflé dish

To make the chocolate sauce: It will hold while you are preparing the soufflé—which will not hold. Put the grated chocolate, sugar, and water in a saucepan. Cook over low heat, stirring often, for about 20 minutes. The sauce should barely simmer. Just before serving, stir in the vanilla and serve hot.

Preheat the oven to 425°F.

To make the soufflé: Slowly heat the milk with the vanilla bean (if you are using vanilla, add it later) in a heavy saucepan. Remove the vanilla bean. Add the grated chocolate and butter, and stir rapidly with a whisk over medium heat. When the sauce has thickened and is smooth, remove the saucepan from the heat. Add the hot water, stirring. If using vanilla, add it now. Beat the egg yolks with the salt and sugar until light. Stir this into the sauce and continue to stir constantly for about 4 minutes. When ready, the mixture should look smooth and satiny. Let it cool briefly.

Rinse each soufflé dish with hot water and quickly dry so they stay warm. Butter each one with about ¼ teaspoon of softened butter, and leave them on the stove to keep warm. Beat the egg whites until stiff but not dry. Pour the chocolate mixture over the whites and fold the two together. Spoon the soufflé batter into the buttered, warm soufflé dishes, filling each about three-fourths full. Put the soufflés in the oven and reduce the heat to 400°F. Bake the soufflés for 12 or 13 minutes. (If making the soufflé in a 2-quart soufflé dish, bake it for 15 to 20 minutes.) Remove the soufflés from the oven and dust the tops with confectioners' sugar.

To make the whipped cream: Whip the cream until nearly stiff. Add the sugar and vanilla and continue beating until the cream is stiff. Serve the chocolate sauce and whipped cream on the side.

NOTE:
When serving a soufflé, place the sauces and whipped cream on the table before removing the soufflé from the oven.

ORANGE SOUFFLÉ WITH ORANGE SAUCE

Although it is a different taste, I like this soufflé just as much as the chocolate soufflé. I stir orange zest preserves into the batter to give it a bit of a chewy texture. As with the chocolate soufflé, you cannot prepare the batter ahead of time and you must take care not to overcook it. Take the soufflé from the oven just before it is done to prevent collapse in the oven. This soufflé can be made either in a soufflé dish or in individual ramekins.

SERVES 4

ORANGE ZEST PRESERVES
  3 oranges
  1 cup water

  ⅓ cup sugar

ORANGE SAUCE
  ⅔ cup fresh orange juice
  Large piece of orange peel

  3 tablespoons sugar

SOUFFLÉ
  1 cup freshly squeezed orange juice
  3 tablespoons sugar
  3 tablespoons butter
  3 tablespoons flour
  3 tablespoons chopped orange zest
    preserves (see above)
  2 egg yolks
  ¼ cup Grand Marnier

  5 egg whites
  ¼ teaspoon salt
  1 to 2 tablespoons confectioners' sugar

  Sweetened Whipped Cream (see
    page 282, but substitute Grand
    Marnier for the vanilla)

To make the preserves: Wash the oranges and use a zester to remove the rind in threads, beginning at the top of the orange and continuing down to the bottom. This method will give you good threads. You should have about ½ cup of zest. Put the zest, water, and sugar in a stainless steel or glass saucepan. Simmer over medium heat for about 30 minutes to make a thick syrup. Remove the pan from the burner and lift the orange zest from the syrup. Lay it on a clean plate until needed for the soufflé.

  To make the orange sauce: Put the orange juice, peel, and sugar in a saucepan. Bring to a boil and cook for 10 minutes. Remove the zest and set aside. Reheat the sauce when you are ready to serve it with the soufflé.

To make the soufflé: Put the orange juice and sugar in a nonaluminum saucepan. Bring to a simmer, cook for 5 minutes, and set aside. Put the butter in another nonaluminum pan, and melt it just a little. Add the flour. Stir well, and cook for a few seconds to melt the butter without browning it. Add the orange juice and cook for a few minutes more, stirring continuously. Remove the pan from the burner. Chop the orange zest from the preserves into small but not tiny pieces to measure 3 tablespoons. Stir them into the batter. If you have leftover preserves, use them to garnish the finished soufflé.

Preheat the oven to 400°F.

Beat the egg yolks slightly and stir them into the orange batter. Add 3 tablespoons of the Grand Marnier and mix well again. Set aside to cool a bit.

Complete the soufflé by beating the egg whites until foamy. Add the salt and continue beating until they form soft peaks, but do not let them become dry and stiff—they should be well beaten yet smooth and soft. Pour the batter into the beaten egg whites. Fold the egg whites to incorporate them into the batter, but do not overfold—don't worry if the batter does not look uniform. Spoon the batter into a buttered 2-quart soufflé dish. It should be three-fourths full. Bake for 15 minutes. The batter can also be baked in four 8-ounce ramekins for 10 to 12 minutes. Watch the baking carefully, making sure not to overcook.

After you have removed the soufflé from the oven, drizzle 1 tablespoon of Grand Marnier over it and then sprinkle with the confectioners' sugar. Serve right away with orange sauce and the sweetened whipped cream. You can also garnish the baked soufflé with the remaining orange zest preserves.

Coconut Layer Cake with Lemon Filling

I nearly always make this cake with a lemon filling—the same filling I make for lemon meringue pie, by the way—and then frost it with a boiled icing generously sprinkled with grated fresh coconut. Coconut cake became popular in the South. Coconuts were common, especially during the winter months; perhaps ships docking in the Deep South brought them from the islands and they became familiar in markets throughout the region. When you buy a coconut, always select one that feels heavy and that obviously has water inside it. Dry coconuts may not be good or have much flavor. To be on the safe side, I suggest buying two coconuts in case one is bad; it is sometimes hard to judge until you have opened them.

The cake itself has a very light texture—helped in part by the beaten egg whites in the batter. Still, no matter how light a batter is, if you overbake it, the cake will be dry and tough. You have to know the moment the cake is ready to be taken from the oven. I use a cake tester but I also listen to the sounds of the cake after it has cooked for 25 minutes. When it is still baking and not yet ready, the liquids make bubbling noises. Just as the cake is done, the sounds become faint and weak, but they should disappear. Sometimes when I take a cake from the oven, I'll think the sounds are not quiet enough, and so I put the cake back for just a minute. And then all the sounds will be gone after that minute! The cake should be soft and springy, as well, and should not smell at all of raw batter. I never leave a cake in the pan to cool but turn it out right away; otherwise it will continue to cook in the hot pan.

There have been times when I have a little trouble with the boiled white icing. No matter how the sugar syrup may look in the pan, you have to keep lifting it on a spoon to check for when it is ready to add to the egg white. I always have the egg white beating in a mixer alongside the stove and try to time it so that it reaches the soft peak stage or becomes white just about the same time the syrup falls from the spoon in a feathery thread about 2 to 3 inches long. If the thread has a ball at the end, the syrup needs more cooking. When the syrup is ready, take it off the heat right away and add it slowly to the egg white while beating on high speed. If you follow the directions carefully, this icing should be easy to make.

MAKES ONE 8-INCH LAYER CAKE

LEMON FILLING

1 cup sugar

¼ teaspoon salt

¼ cup water

½ cup lemon juice, strained through a fine strainer

1 tablespoon butter

5 beaten egg yolks

CAKE

½ cup (1 stick) unsalted butter

1 cup superfine sugar

2 cups unbleached all-purpose flour

¼ teaspoon salt

5 teaspoons single-acting baking powder (see page 208)

1 cup milk, at room temperature

1 teaspoon vanilla

1 teaspoon freshly squeezed lemon juice

4 egg whites

WHITE BOILED ICING

1 fresh coconut

1 egg white

½ cup granulated sugar

2 tablespoons cold water

½ teaspoon vanilla

To make the filling: Put the sugar, salt, water, and lemon juice into a 2-quart nonaluminum saucepan, and set over medium heat. Stir until the sugar is completely dissolved. Have the beaten egg yolks in a bowl. Pour some of the hot mixture into the bowl, stirring the yolks as you pour to prevent them from curdling. Pour the yolk mixture back into the saucepan and return it to the stove. Cook carefully, stirring continuously, until the contents become translucent and will definitely coat a spoon. Then mix in the butter. Let this mixture cool; overnight is best.

To make the cake: Put the butter in the large bowl of an electric mixer and beat until it becomes waxy. Add the sugar and beat again. All of this

(recipe continues)

should be done at medium speed. Blend until the mixture becomes light and fluffy—do not be impatient. Now mix one-fourth of the flour with the salt and baking powder, and mix into the batter. Then add one-fourth of the milk and mix again. Continue to add flour, then milk, until all the milk is used. Finish with the last of the flour. Mix well, then add the vanilla and lemon juice.

Beat the egg whites to firm soft peaks and fold them lightly into the batter. Butter the bottoms of two 8-inch cake pans and then lightly dust them with flour. Spoon the batter into the prepared cake pans. If you have kitchen scales, it is good to weigh the pans of batter to see that they contain equal amounts. Set in a preheated 375°F oven to bake for 20 to 25 minutes. Check after 20 minutes to listen for quiet sounds. If there are none, remove the cake from the oven and turn out onto a wire rack to cool. It is also ready when a cake tester comes out of the center of a layer clean and when there is no raw batter smell. When the cake layers are cool, cover them with a clean, odor-free cloth until you are ready to fill and ice.

When you are ready to fill and ice the cake, put the bottom cake layer on a serving dish. Stir the filling well so that it is easy to spread. You may not need all of the filling for the cake. You can save the rest for another use, such as little tarts. It will keep in the refrigerator for 4 to 5 days. After you have finished spreading the filling, position the second layer on top of the first. Then prepare the icing.

To make the boiled icing: Use only a coconut with good flavor. To break open the coconut, use a hammer, striking through the middle. Hold the coconut over the sink for draining the water. With a stout knife make a cut in the flesh the shape of a pie slice and then pry out the pieces. Peel off the brown skin. Grate the coconut pieces on a four-sided grater using the fine side. After grating the coconut, you should have about 3 cups. Set aside until the icing is ready.

Set the mixer or mixing bowl near the stove. Put the egg white in the mixing bowl or the bowl of an electric mixer and beat it just until foamy. In a saucepan over medium heat, bring the sugar and water to a boil without stirring. When the syrup comes to a full boil, watch your time very carefully. One minute after the syrup comes to a boil, begin to beat the egg whites. After about 2 minutes, begin to test the boiling syrup. Dip the side of a spoon into the syrup and hold it above the pan. The thread you are waiting to see will hang from the spoon and be a clear filament of at least 2 or 3 inches. If the thread has a ball on its end, then it is not ready. Continue to cook and dip the spoon into the syrup until the thread appears. You do not want to overcook the syrup as it will get a grainy texture. As soon as the thread appears, take the pan from the heat.

Quickly finish beating the egg white until it holds its shape. Slowly pour the hot syrup into the beaten white and continue beating the mixture until the icing falls in peaks or holds its shape. Let the frosting cool for a few minutes, then add the vanilla and mix well.

Spoon a generous amount of the icing on the center of the cake, and frost the top and the sides. Make sure the cake is well covered. Sprinkle the grated coconut in a thick layer over the top and sides of the cake.

CHOCOLATE ICED LAYER CAKE

I think of this cake as a Sunday cake because, for some reason, it is common throughout the South to serve a yellow layer cake iced with chocolate to company. It is a simple cake to make, but as with all cakes, be careful not to overbake it or it will be tough and dry. Everyone loves this cake, especially children, who just seem to adore anything made with chocolate. The icing is very chocolaty and quick to prepare. I guessed at it the first time and now find that it is the easiest kind of icing to make come out smooth. And it tastes so good.

MAKES ONE 9-INCH LAYER CAKE

LAYER CAKE

¾ cup (1½ sticks) butter, at room
temperature
1½ cups superfine sugar
3 whole eggs
3 cups unbleached all-purpose flour,
sifted

1 teaspoon salt
2 tablespoons single-acting baking
powder (see page 208)
1 cup milk, at room temperature
1 tablespoon vanilla

CHOCOLATE ICING

1 cup granulated sugar
1 tablespoon butter
3 ounces (3 squares) unsweetened
chocolate

1 cup heavy cream (not ultra-
pasteurized), warmed
Pinch salt
2 teaspoons vanilla

To make the layer cake: Put the butter in the bowl of an electric mixer and beat on medium speed until it becomes waxy. Add the sugar and beat until the mixture becomes light in texture. Add 1 egg and beat until it is well absorbed. Add the other 2 eggs and beat again. Toss the flour with the salt and baking powder. Mix a bit of it into the batter and then add a fourth of the milk and blend well. Continue blending, first some flour and then some milk, ending with flour, until both are used up. Add the vanilla and mix well again. Now give the batter a good beating with a stout wooden spoon to make sure that it is scraped up from the bottom of the bowl and well mixed.

Butter and flour two 9-inch cake pans and spoon equal amounts of batter into each one. (You can weigh them to see that they are equal.) Set the cakes to bake on the middle rack of a preheated 375°F oven for 20 to 25 minutes, until the sounds of the cake slow down (see Coconut Layer Cake instructions, page 286), and a cake tester inserted in the center of a layer comes out clean. The cake should not smell at all of raw dough and will be beginning to pull away from the sides of the pan. Turn the cake layers out of the pans right away onto wire racks to cool while you prepare the icing.

To make the icing: Put the sugar, butter, and chocolate in a 1-quart saucepan, and set it over hot water to melt. When melted, remove from the heat and gently stir in the heavy cream and salt. Set over a medium burner, bring to a lively boil, and cook until the mixture forms a soft ball when dropped into cold water. Remove the icing from the burner and add the vanilla. Stir the icing, let it cool for 12 minutes, and then give it a really good stir.

When the cake layers are cool and the icing is the right temperature and consistency to spread, place the bottom cake layer on a serving plate. Spread the icing on the top of the bottom layer. Gently place the top layer over this. Use the remaining icing to spread over the top and sides of the cake.

SMALL CAKES

The batter for these cakes is very, very short, which means they have lots of shortening and no leavener. The result is that they have the crumbly texture of traditional shortbread but the appearance of a cupcake, since they are baked in deep muffin tins. I usually serve them with ice cream, fruit, or ices.

MAKES 24 CAKES

2 cups unbleached all-purpose flour

1 cup (2 sticks) unsalted butter

¼ cup granulated sugar

1 teaspoon salt

1 rounded teaspoon ground ginger

Confectioners' sugar (optional)

Preheat the oven to 350°F.

Put all of the ingredients except the confectioners' sugar in a mixing bowl. Blend until the mixture becomes ivory colored but do not overblend. This is a light batter and it is raised just by the power of the mixing. Take care not to overmix—as the butter warms up during mixing, it softens and can make the dough too soft. If you don't have a mixer, beat by hand until the dough becomes light in texture. After the dough is well mixed, butter 24 small muffin tins and spoon the dough into them, filling each three-fourths full.

Put the tins in the oven and bake for 15 to 20 minutes, until the cakes are light brown on top. Remove the cakes from the oven and let rest awhile, then turn them onto a wire rack. When cold, dust with confectioners' sugar if you like, or you may serve them as they are. Store in closed tins.

Black Walnut Pound Cake

The very strong, very distinctive taste of black walnuts is better when they are freshly shelled. However, they usually are sold already shelled because the procedure is so difficult—which helps explain why they are so expensive. My aunt used to put the egg-sized nuts on the driveway and let the cars roll over them to crack the green outer shell. Inside is a tough brown husk. You can still buy them unshelled at some roadside stands and health-food stores. If you use English walnuts for this cake, it will be good but won't taste the same.

MAKES ONE 9-INCH TUBE CAKE

1 cup (2 sticks) unsalted butter

1⅔ cups superfine sugar

5 eggs

2 cups less 1 tablespoon unbleached all-purpose flour

1 teaspoon salt

2 teaspoons vanilla

1 cup chopped black walnuts

Put the butter in a mixing bowl, and beat on medium speed until the butter becomes waxy. Add the sugar gradually. Beat until the mixture becomes white and light in texture. Drop in one whole egg at a time, beating after each addition. Mix in half of the flour, then add the salt and vanilla, and beat again. Add the rest of the flour, mix thoroughly, then add the black walnuts, and mix well again. Butter and flour the bottom (not the sides) of a 9-inch tube pan, and spoon the batter into it. Set the pan in a cold oven on the center rack. Turn the oven on to 275°F, and bake for 35 minutes. Then increase the heat to 325°F to finish baking for another 15 to 20 minutes, at which time the cake should have risen to the top of the pan and become brown. Remove from the oven and cool in the pan on a wire rack for 15 minutes. When cold, unmold and store in a tin lined with wax paper.

WHISKEY CAKE

Heavy cakes such as this one are common in the South for holidays and other special occasions, partly because they keep so well under a covered dish (but not a plastic cake dome). The cake keeps for quite a few days and often is sliced and toasted and then eaten with ice cream or brandied peaches as a snack or quick dessert. I use a tube pan to bake it, although you could make it oblong. As to what kind of bourbon you should use, I would never use a bourbon I would not drink. The Brazil nuts, which used to be more popular than they are today, add to its richness—they're really good. You could use English walnuts and they might have even stronger flavor. I grind all nuts in a little hand grinder; it doesn't squeeze the oils out. Sometimes I think the motors of electric appliances get too hot and change the flavor of the nuts as they chop them.

MAKES ONE 10-INCH TUBE CAKE

1 cup (2 sticks) unsalted butter

1⅔ cups superfine sugar

4 whole eggs plus 1 egg yolk

12 ounces (3 cups) unbleached all-purpose flour

½ teaspoon salt

½ teaspoon ground mace

1 tablespoon single-acting baking powder (see page 208)

1 cup bourbon

8 ounces Brazil nuts, ground

Butter the bottom only of a 10-inch tube pan.

In a bowl or an electric mixer set on medium speed, beat the butter until it becomes waxy. Add the sugar, and beat until the mixture becomes very light in texture. Add the eggs and yolk one at a time, beating well after each addition. Add 1 cup of flour with the salt, mace, and baking powder, mixing well again. Gradually add the bourbon, alternating with remaining flour until both are used up. Mix well, stir in the ground nuts, and pour the batter into the prepared tube pan. Set in a cold oven. Turn on the oven to 275°F for 30 minutes. Then raise the oven to 300°F for 30 minutes, and finally raise it to 325°F for 15 minutes. Remove from the oven and turn out onto a wire rack to cool. Wrap in wax paper when cold and store in a clean tin in a cool, dry place.

MERINGUE SHELLS

It took me a long time to get meringues right. Some people cook them and leave them in a turned-off oven overnight. I've tried this and for my taste they become over-crisp. I find the most satisfactory way to make meringues is to set them in a cold oven, turn the oven on to 250°F, and bake them for 1 hour. Then, turn the oven off and leave the meringues in it for another hour. Some cooks also say that beating the egg whites by hand incorporates more air into them than beating them with an electric mixer. I find that the KitchenAid, turned to the highest speed, does a good job. Having the whites at room temperature ensures success but I add the cream of tartar just to make sure nothing goes wrong. I beat the whites and cream of tartar until they are thick and white and then I add the sugar. When you bite into a meringue, it should be crisp all the way through, not just on the outside, which I think happens during that extra hour in the shut-off oven. I do not pay any attention to the humidity of the day when I make meringues, and I store them for 3 or 4 days in a tin can with a tight-fitting cover without any loss to taste or texture. I suggest serving these, which are flavored with hazelnuts, with sliced peaches, berries, and some custard sauce.

MAKES 8 TO 10 SHELLS

4 egg whites
¼ teaspoon cream of tartar
1 cup superfine sugar

½ cup coarsely chopped hazelnuts

First, prepare a cookie sheet with parchment paper. Do not grease the parchment; you will be able to remove the shells easily after baking. Using an electric mixer or hand beater, beat the egg whites and cream of tartar until they are white and thick. Then lower the speed and add the sugar. Speed up again and beat until the egg whites stand up firmly when the beater is removed. Sprinkle in the chopped hazelnuts and gently fold them into the meringue. Have two teaspoons ready nearby. With a large spoon, dip out enough meringue onto the parchment to make a nest about 3 inches in diameter. Place the nests 1½ inches apart as they do tend to spread a little during baking. Using the two teaspoons, shape the meringues into nests with depressed centers. Do not

(recipe continues)

make the depressions too wide or deep or the walls of the meringue will be too thin.

Set the meringues in a cold oven, then turn the heat to 250°F and bake for 1 hour. Turn off the oven at this time and let the meringues sit there for another hour. Test for doneness. Try not to overbrown; the meringues should be an ivory color. When cooked, remove from the oven and leave them to cool on the pan. Remove the meringues with a spatula and store them in a tin with a tight cover until needed.

Rich Floating Island with Raspberry Preserves and Spun Sugar

The custard in this recipe, which is very rich, is one I developed on the spot one day when I was making floating island for some people who did not have enough milk. I used cream and half-and-half as well as some milk, and the custard came out just wonderfully. It also has vanilla and almond extracts, which you have to be careful with. Too much added liquid will break down the custard. I added the raspberry preserves and spun sugar to dress up the dessert, but you don't have to. When I was young, floating island was a common dessert. Just as with Tyler pie, everyone always had the ingredients and it was easy to make.

SERVES 4

RICH CUSTARD

2 cups milk	½ vanilla bean, split down 1 inch
½ cup heavy cream (not ultra-pasteurized)	½ cup sugar
	4 egg yolks
1 cup half-and-half	2 teaspoons vanilla
¼ rounded teaspoon salt	1 teaspoon almond extract

TOPPING

3 egg whites	½ teaspoon vanilla
3 tablespoons sugar	½ cup homemade raspberry preserves
Pinch salt	Spun Sugar (see page 299) (optional)
¼ teaspoon almond extract	

Put the milk, cream, half-and-half, salt, vanilla bean, and sugar in a 1½-quart saucepan. Stir well and set over a medium burner to reach the scalding point, that is, the point just before boiling. Beat the egg yolks slightly in a bowl. Remove the vanilla bean from the scalded milk and pour some of the scalded milk into the beaten yolks, stirring all the while to keep the eggs from cooking. Then pour the egg mixture into the saucepan. Return it to a low burner, and stir while cooking, until custard coats the back of a spoon (about 8 min-

(recipe continues)

utes). Remove from the burner and set the saucepan into a pan of cold water to halt any further cooking. Strain this custard through a fine sieve and add the vanilla and almond extracts. Set aside to cool. Put the custard in an open ovenproof dish.

Before the dinner is served, make the topping. Beat the egg whites until they become white and thick, then add the sugar, salt, almond extract, and vanilla. Continue to beat until the whites stand in peaks. Spoon the beaten whites onto the custard, making as many islands as you have guests. Leave a bit of space between each island. Dot each island with ½ teaspoon of preserves and set in a preheated 375°F oven for a few minutes, just until the islands are light brown. Then cover with spun sugar, if you choose to. Once assembled, the dessert can sit in the kitchen through dinner, until you are ready to serve.

SPUN SUGAR

The trick to making spun sugar is to keep the melted sugar warm by setting it over very hot water, which is why it is a good idea to make it standing near the stove so that you can heat the water in the pan or keep a kettle full of simmering water to add to the pan. I don't have fancy equipment. I just take a broomstick and lay it between two chairs and then use a fork to move the strands of sugar back and forth over the broomstick. I once took a piece of wire and twisted it all around for lots of tines, but mostly I use a fork. It's kind of fun to make spun sugar and in no time you have enough for a little nest.

MAKES ENOUGH FOR 4 SMALL "NESTS"
OR TOPS

1 cup sugar

Position a clean broomstick or long rolling pin between two chairs or similar objects so that the broomstick is suspended 3 or 4 feet above the floor.

Put the sugar in a heavy saucepan and place it over medium heat. Watch the sugar carefully and take it from the stove as soon as it melts and turns a golden amber color. Do not stir it as it melts. Set the pan in another pan partially filled with very hot, not boiling, water. Choose a fork with a good

(recipe continues)

number of tines and dip it into the syrup. Raise the fork above the pan. There will be amber threads streaming from the fork. Carefully lay the threads over the stick by waving the fork back and forth above it so that the threads fall down either side. Repeat this process until you have spun enough of the sugar in this way. Gather the still-warm threads together with both hands and form them into a rounded shape large enough to cover the dish you are decorating. The warm sugar is easy to bend and should not be so brittle that it breaks. Store the spun sugar in an airtight container or use it right away. You may choose to make individual nests of spun sugar to cover small tarts or other desserts.

PLUM PUDDING

Although I have never used a recipe that actually has plums, old English recipes for plum pudding sometimes include whole plums and even a leg of mutton, all chopped up. Mine is a scaled-down version of the heavier, denser puddings that are so often thought of when plum pudding is mentioned. For a lot of people, this is a pleasant surprise because my pudding does not have all kinds of different dried fruits or too much brandy, so it is light and delicious. There is enough brandy for flavor and preserving, so you can, if you want, make the pudding in October and keep it in the refrigerator until Christmas, when you steam it again before serving it with Nutmeg Sauce.

SERVES 8 TO 10

8 ounces seedless raisins	1 teaspoon single-acting baking powder
4 ounces almonds	(see page 208)
8 ounces currants	1 teaspoon ground cinnamon
¾ cup brandy	⅓ nutmeg, grated
4 ounces suet, cut from veal kidney fat	¼ teaspoon ground mace
½ cup fine bread crumbs	⅔ cup milk, scalded
1½ cups (packed) dark brown sugar	3 egg yolks, lightly beaten
¼ cup flour	3 egg whites
1 scant teaspoon salt	Sprig of holly, for decoration
	Nutmeg Sauce (see page 251)

The day before you will be making the pudding, cut the raisins in half and grate the almonds. Put them in a small bowl with the currants and pour ½ cup of the brandy over. Stir and then cover the bowl tightly.

The next day, chop the suet after cutting away any skin or veins. Finely chopped suet is as smooth as any shortening and the fat from veal kidneys not only has the right consistency but is sweet, too. Put the chopped suet in a large mixing bowl and add the bread crumbs and brown sugar. Combine the flour with the salt and baking powder and mix with the suet. Next, add the cinnamon, grated nutmeg, and mace. When these ingredients are well combined, stir in the scalded milk. Continue to stir the mixture and add the egg yolks and the brandied fruit and nuts. Mix well.

(recipe continues)

Beat the egg whites until stiff and then thoroughly but gently fold them into the pudding. Cover the bowl and set the pudding in a cool place overnight.

Grease a 1½-quart mold or three 1-pint molds by rubbing all around with suet. Fill it (or them) two-thirds full with the pudding and cover tightly. Set a round cake rack in the bottom of a large kettle and add enough water to cover the mold. Bring the water to a boil and put the mold in the kettle. When the water returns to the boil, reduce the heat and simmer for 2½ hours.

Cool the mold on a rack. If using a metal mold, take the cooled pudding from it and wrap it in wax or parchment paper and then foil. If using a porcelain mold, leave the pudding in the mold. Store the pudding in a cool place or the bottom of the refrigerator. Two hours before serving, put the pudding, still wrapped or still in the mold, in the top of a double boiler set over simmering water. Cover, and let the pudding steam for 2 hours. Carefully remove the pudding from the mold or wrapping by tilting and sliding it onto a serving dish. Decorate with holly. Heat the remaining ¼ cup of brandy in a small saucepan and, just before serving the pudding, pour the hot brandy over the pudding and light it. Serve with Nutmeg Sauce.

BAKING COOKIES

You should have plenty of time for cookies. I usually don't plan to eat them the same day I make them because I think most are better if you leave the dough for a day to dry out before baking. They just come out much better. With some cookies, if you roll them out, cut them, and put the cookie sheet right in the oven the cookies will just go "squash." If you hold them for a day before you bake them, they keep their shape. Either leave the dough in the bowl or roll it out and cut it. You don't have to refrigerate it (although you can); just put it in a cool room.

I always like to use heavy cookie sheets. If the sheets are too thin the cookies will burn, and there is the risk that the cookie sheets will warp with time. You can buy cookie sheets with a layer of insulation between the top and the bottom, but as good as these are, they are expensive and often quite small. Look for heavy-gauge metal rimless cookie sheets. A rim makes it hard to lift the cookies off the sheet.

NUT BUTTER BALLS

Nut Butter Balls are the cookies everyone likes and they're easy to make, too. I use pecans or walnuts, but I prefer pecans. Walnut skins are sometimes a little bitter, and for my taste, it is not worth the trouble removing the skins. These cookies are better if you let the dough sit overnight before baking. You roll the cookies in vanilla sugar while they are still warm, and for this you need about 3 cups, but I suggest making at least 4 cups of vanilla sugar at a time and keeping it for other recipes. It is simple to make—just bury a split vanilla bean in a cannister of granulated sugar. It needs to ripen at least 1 week before using.

MAKES ABOUT 4 DOZEN BALLS

6 to 7 ounces pecans

2 cups unbleached all-purpose flour

1 cup (2 sticks) unsalted butter, softened

¼ cup granulated sugar

Pinch salt

1 teaspoon almond extract

1 teaspoon vanilla

3 cups vanilla sugar (see above)

Put the nuts through a nut grater and measure—you will need 1½ cups. Handle lightly so as not to pack down. Sift the flour once. Beat the butter and sugar together until the texture becomes creamy. Add the salt and flavorings and mix well again. Beat at a low speed, gradually adding the flour. When the flour has been mixed in, add the nuts and beat until the batter lightens and becomes a grayish color—about 4 minutes. Spoon the dough into a bowl, cover, and put in the refrigerator overnight to chill.

The next morning, preheat the oven to 400°F. Remove the bowl from the refrigerator and shape the dough into 1-inch balls, using a melon scoop. Place the balls on ungreased cookie sheets and bake for 12 minutes. Check the balls to be sure they are not browning. If they seem soft, let them bake for another minute or two, but do not let them brown or they will be dry. Take the balls from the oven and leave them on the cookie sheets for 5 minutes or more before removing them with a spatula to a wire rack. Let them cool about 15 minutes or more. Then roll them in the vanilla sugar and let them cool before storing them in a clean, dry tin.

SPECIAL SUGAR COOKIES FOR DECORATING

These are not as rich as the Nut Butter Balls but are just the right consistency for decorating for Christmas. Crushed sugar cubes will not dissolve while baking and are perfect for decorating, giving a snowy white finish. To cut the cookie shapes, use 1½- to 2-inch cutters shaped any way you like—rounds, stars, crescents—and be sure to cut the cookies so that there is very little dough between each one. The dough loses its taste and texture if scraps are rerolled and recut. I suggest baking the cookies in thirds and keeping the unused dough in the refrigerator. The dough is very soft and is difficult to roll in larger amounts or if it sits too long at room temperature. However, you may roll all the dough at once between two sheets of parchment. Cut the rolled-out dough in half and refrigerate one half while baking the other. Watch the cookies carefully as they bake and take them from the oven when they are very lightly browned. If they turn any darker, more than a tan color, the flavor will change and they will not be as good. Something about the browning changes things.

MAKES ABOUT 50 COOKIES

½ cup (1 stick) unsalted butter
¾ cup superfine sugar
2 medium eggs
2 cups unbleached all-purpose flour
1½ teaspoons ground ginger
½ teaspoon single-acting baking powder
   (see page 208)
1 tablespoon cream
½ cup crushed sugar cubes (see page 223)

Cream together the butter, sugar, and eggs, mixing well. Sift the flour with the ginger and baking powder and add that to the batter. Add the cream and mix well. Spoon the dough onto a dinner plate (the dough will be very soft) and spread it evenly over the plate. Let this rest for 45 minutes in the freezer or overnight in the refrigerator. It is important that this very soft dough be well chilled; your rolling board should also be put in the refrigerator, if possible.

(recipe continues)

Remove one-third of the dough, putting the rest back in the refrigerator to keep it nice and cold. Flour the rolling surface and the rolling pin. Roll the dough quickly so that it is as thin as possible, about the thickness of a quarter; these cookies taste best when they are rolled thin. Next, cut them with 1½- to 2-inch cookie cutters in any shape you want. Cut out the shapes very close to one another so you don't waste the dough. Rerolling the dough is a wasted effort; the texture and taste will change. Either bake the trimmings or discard them. Lift the cookies onto an ungreased cookie sheet with a spatula. If some of the cookies are rolled thinner than others, put the thin ones in the center of the cookie sheet. Repeat with the remaining dough, baking two batches together if you have room. Sprinkle the cookies in decorative ways with the crushed sugar cubes. Put the sugar on so that the cookies will look pretty on a tray or in a gift box. Place them in a preheated 400°F oven for 8 to 10 minutes, until they are a delicate pale brown. The flavor is spoiled if these cookies are too brown. Remove them to a wire rack to cool, then store them in a clean, dry tin.

BUTTER COOKIES

Though I always make these cookies for Christmas, they are good the whole year through. The other cookies given here are fancy but these are plain—no decorations, no nuts; just simple, good cookies.

MAKES 3 DOZEN

1 cup (2 sticks) butter, softened
½ cup superfine sugar
1 egg yolk, lightly beaten

½ teaspoon vanilla
½ teaspoon almond extract
1¾ cups unbleached all-purpose flour

Cream the butter until it is shiny and light in color. Add the sugar gradually to the butter and beat until the mixture becomes light and fluffy. Add the egg yolk and mix until the texture is smooth, then mix in the vanilla and almond extracts and combine well. Turn the mixer on low and gradually add the flour in large spoonfuls until well blended and light in texture. Spoon the batter into a cookie press and form whatever simple shapes you prefer. If you push the cookie press against the cookie sheet as you exert pressure, you will get a thicker cookie. Give each cookie enough room so as not to touch, spacing them ¾ inch apart. Put the cookies in the refrigerator overnight or set them in a cold room overnight.

The next day, bake the cookies in a preheated 375°F oven for 10 to 12 minutes, until they are lightly browned. Overbrowning tends to dry the cookies out. These are very rich cookies. Let them cool for a few minutes, then carefully remove them to a wire rack to cool. If the cookies remain on the cookie sheet too long, they will harden and break when they are removed. If this should occur, just put them back in the oven for a few minutes. When cooled, place them in a clean tin lined with wax paper and close tightly until ready to use.

INDEX

appetizers
    grilled eggplant with marinated
        tomatoes and artichokes, 36–7
    herring roe, 154
    pork liver pâté, 117–18
    rabbit pâté, 130–1
    shrimp paste, 151
    white eggplant slices with tomato and
        onion sauce, 35
    see also hors d'oeuvres
apple(s)
    baked Staymen Winesap, with rich
        custard sauce, 276
    brown betty, 275
    chutney, 183
    glazed, for side dish or stuffing,
        111–12
    lady, 185
        pickled, 177, 185
        spiced, 185
    marinated apple tart with custard
        sauce, 271–3
artichokes
    Jerusalem, 177, 199
        pickled, 199–200
    marinated, grilled eggplant with, 36–7

bacon, 65, 124 (box)
    in pâtés, 117, 124, 130
    smoked vs. fresh, 124

baking powder
    double-acting vs. single-acting, 207
    making your own, 208
baking soda, curdling of milk prevented
    by, 21
bananas, sautéed, 57
barley beef stew, 47–8
Bartlett pears, 181, 274
basil, 7, 21, 28 (box)
    purple, 28 (box)
batter bread, 206
    corn, light, 227
batter cakes, corn, 226
beans
    dried, 49 (box), 52
        black-eyed peas in tomato and
            onion sauce, 50
        thirteen-bean soup, 51
        white, and lentils in tomato
            sauce, 52
    green
        canned, in pork stock, 20
        long-cooked, 19
        in salad of whole tomatoes, 27–8
        in summer hot vegetable dish,
            30–1
béarnaise sauce, 136–7
beef, 66
    barley stew, 47–8
    mincemeat tarts with brandy butter,
        268–70

beef (continued)
    soup with wild mushrooms, 47, 48
    tenderloin with béarnaise sauce,
        136–7
benne (sesame) seed biscuits, 209
berries, 177, 178
    freezing, 252 (box)
    storing, 81
    summer pudding, 241–2
    wild, 189 (box)
    see also blackberries; boysenberries;
        elderberries; gooseberries;
        raspberries; strawberries
biscuits, 205–6
    benne (sesame) seed, 209
    buttermilk or sour milk, 212–13
    storing and reheating, 209–10
    for two or three, 210
blackberry(ies), 177
    freezing, 252 (box)
    jelly, 192–3
    pie, 261
    roly-poly, 253–4
    summer pudding, 241–2
    wild, 189, 192–3
black-eyed peas, 49
    in tomato and onion sauce, 50
black walnut pound cake, 293
blueberries, 177
    freezing, 252 (box)
boysenberry(ies), 261
    jelly, 192–3
    pie, 261
brandied orange sauce, 103–4
brandy butter, 268–70
Brazil nut whiskey cake, 294
bread, 205–7
    cardamom, 222–3
    Christmas stollen, 229–30
    coffee cake, 232–3
    Ethiopian, 221
    nut, 231
    popovers, 215–16
    storing, 81
    see also batter bread; biscuits; corn
        bread; spoon bread; yeast bread
brown betty, apple, 275
Brunswick stew, 94–5

butter
    brandy or rum, 268–70
    shallot, 149
butter cookies, 307
buttermilk, 206–7, 211 (box)
    biscuits, 212–13
butter pie pastry, 256–7
    shells, 258

cabbage, 53 (box); *see also* sauerkraut
cake(s), 286–94
    black walnut pound, 293
    chocolate iced layer, 290–1
    coconut layer, with lemon filling,
        286–9
    coffee, 232–3
    small, 292
    storing, 81
    whiskey, 294
canning, *see* home canning
caramel sauce, for ice cream, 246
cardamom bread, 222–3
carrots, in summer hot vegetable dish,
    30–1
catfish
    fried, 156
    stew, 156
cèpes, field, 44
Charleston-style she-crab soup, 166
cheese, 64
    custard, 71
    soufflé, 72
    straws, 214
cherries
    canned, 177
    Royal Ann, 177, 182
chervil,
chestnuts, 58, 278 (box)
    braised, 58
    with chocolate glaze, 277
    cleaning and preparing, 278
    in heavy syrup, 201
    purée of, 59
chicken, 66, 74–85
    breast
        in parchment, 83–4
        sautéed, 85

icing, cake
    chocolate, 290–1
    white boiled, 287–8

jams, 177–8
    sealing jars with paraffin, 194
    see also preserves
jelly(ies), 177–8, 189 (box)
    blackberry or boysenberry, 192–3
    elderberry, guava, or wild grape, 193
    sealing jars with paraffin, 194
jelly bags, homemade, 191 (box)
Jerusalem artichokes, 177, 199
    pickled, 199–200
Jolof rice, 54

Keiffer pears, 177
    canned, 181
    chutney, 183
Kentucky Wonder beans, long-cooked, 19
kidneys, veal, sautéed, 107
Kirby cucumbers, pickled, 197–8

lady apples, 185
    pickled, 177, 185
        spiced, 185
lamb, 66
    roast boneless leg of, 106
lard, 206–7, 260 (box)
    pie pastry, 259
leek(s)
    cleaning, 42
    and potato soup, 42
    steamed leaves of, 43
    in summer hot vegetable dish, 30–1
lemon filling, for layer cake, 287
lentils, white beans with, in tomato
        sauce, 52
lettuce, wilted, salad, 24
liver pâté, pork, 117–18

mackerel, broiled, 173
mango chutney, 183
mashed potatoes, *see* whipped potatoes

mayonnaise, 29
    herb, 29
    light, for crabmeat, 168–9
    oils used for, 14
    olive, 143
meat, 64–6
    buying, 66
    fresh vs. frozen, 65, 66
    in Red Rice, 54–5
    storing, 65, 66, 81
    see also beef; chicken; duck; ham;
        lamb; pork; rabbit; turkey; veal
meringue shells, 295–6
milk
    curdling prevented by baking soda, 21
    sour, for baking, 206, 211 (box)
mincemeat tarts with brandy butter,
        268–70
morels
    in oil, 13
    in pastry shells, boiled eggs on, 70
    sautéed, 44
mushrooms
    morels in oil, 13
    in pastry shells, boiled eggs on, 70
    sautéed, 44
        in summer hot vegetable dish, 30–1
    wild, 13, 44
        beef soup with, 48
        sautéed, 44
mustard greens, in cooked greens, 17–18
mustard with brown sugar, 122

nut(s)
    black walnut pound cake, 293
    Brazil nut whiskey cake, 294
    bread, 231
    meringue shells, 295–6
    pecan butter ball cookies, 304
    pralines, 279
    see also chestnuts
nut butter balls, 304
nutmeg sauce, 251

oil, use of, 14
okra, whipped cornmeal with, 38

whole, salad of, garnished with green
        beans and scallions, 27–8
trout, panfried, 172
turkey
    roast stuffed, 86–7
    wild, roast, 88–9
Tyler pie, 265

vanilla-flavored sweetened whipped
        cream, 282–3
vanilla ice cream, old-fashioned custard-
        based, 243–4
veal, 66
    kidneys, sautéed, 107
vegetable oil, 14
vegetables, 5–7
    cooking time, 5, 19
    pickling, 177, 195–200
    sausage baked in pastry with, 126–7
    storing, 81
    summer hot dish of, 30–1
    see also artichokes; beans; cabbage;
        carrots; corn; cucumbers;
        cymling; eggplant; greens; leeks;
        mushrooms; okra; onions; peas;
        potatoes; pumpkin; salsify;
        spinach; tomatoes; watercress;
        zucchini
Vidalia onions, 10, 177, 195
    fresh green peas with, 10
    pickled, 195–6
vinaigrette, 27–8
Virginia ham, 65, 119, 120–1, 123
    boiled, 119–20

kinds of, 120
mustard for, 122
poached eggs on slices of, 68
potatoes baked with, 40
Virginia spots, panfried, 155

walnut
    bread, 231
    black, pound cake, 293
watercress
    soup, 16
    wild, cooked in pork stock, 15
    wild vs. cultivated, 15
whipped cream, see cream
whipped potatoes, 41
    sauerkraut and pork sausage with,
        128
whiskey cake, 294
Williamsburg ham, 120
wilted lettuce salad, 24

yams, 46
yeast bread, 206–7, 219–24
    cardamom, 222–3
    Christmas stollen, 229–30
    Ethiopian bread, 221
    hot rolls, 224
    Saturday night, 219–20
yeast rolls, hot, 224

zucchini, in eggplant stew, 33

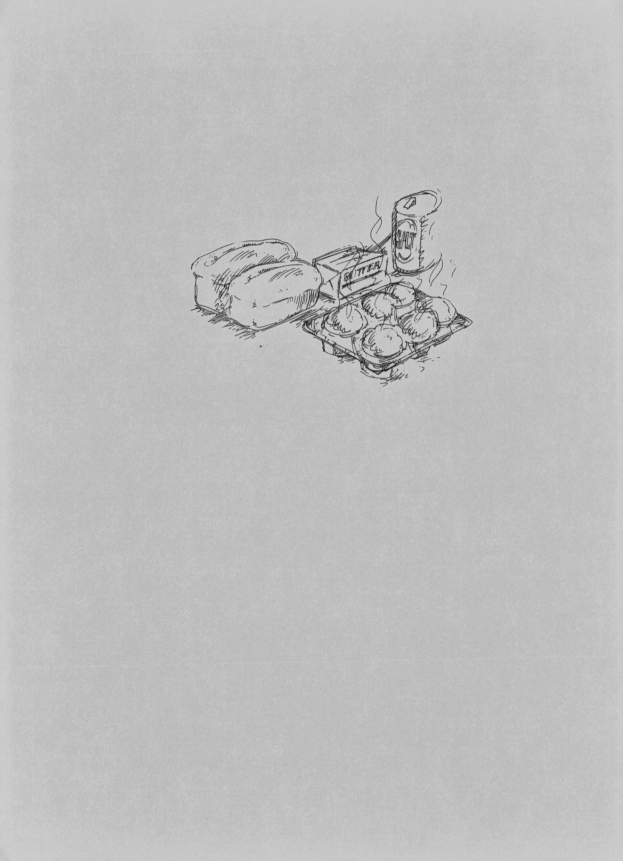

A NOTE ABOUT THE AUTHOR

Edna Lewis was born in Freetown, Virginia, a farming community founded after the Civil War by freed slaves (among them her grandfather). For years she lived in New York, where she started her career at the famed Café Nicholson. Miss Lewis was the recipient of numerous awards, including the inaugural James Beard Living Legend and Southern Foodways Alliance Lifetime Achievement Awards, and the Grande Dame des Dames d'Escoffier International. Together with Scott Peacock, she helped create the Society for the Revival and Preservation of Southern Food. She was also the author of *The Taste of Country Cooking, The Edna Lewis Cookbook,* and, with Scott Peacock, *The Gift of Southern Cooking.* She retired to Decatur, Georgia, where she died in February 2006.

A NOTE ON THE TYPE

The text of this book was set in Sabon, a typeface designed by Jan Tschichold (1902–1974), the well-known German typographer. Designed in 1966 and based on the original designs by Claude Garamond (ca. 1480–1561), Sabon was named for the punch cutter Jacques Sabon, who brought Garamond's matrices to Frankfurt.

Composed by North Market Street Graphics,
Lancaster, Pennsylvania

Printed and bound LSC Communications,
Crawfordsville, Indiana

Designed by M. Kristen Bearse

Edna Lewis was born in 1916 in Freetown, Virginia, a farming community founded after the Civil War by freed slaves (among them her grandfather) and for many years lived and cooked in New York City. She was the recipient of numerous awards, including the inaugural James Beard Living Legend and Southern Foodways Alliance (SFA) Lifetime Achievement Awards, the Grande Dame des Dames d'Escoffier International, and the International Association of Culinary Professionals (IACP) Lifetime Achievement Award. Her books were inducted into the James Beard Foundation Cookbook Hall of Fame, and she was commemorated with a United States Postal Service postage stamp. Miss Lewis was also the author of *The Edna Lewis Cookbook, The Taste of Country Cooking,* and, with Scott Peacock, *The Gift of Southern Cooking.* She died in February 2006.